Selling in Your Comfort Zone

Safe and Effective Strategies for Developing New Business

D1568175

Robert N. Kohn and Lawrence M. Kohn

 **LawPracticeManagementSection**
MARKETING • MANAGEMENT • TECHNOLOGY • FINANCE

Commitment to Quality: The Law Practice Division is committed to quality in our publications. Our authors are experienced practitioners in their fields. Prior to publication, the contents of all our books are rigorously reviewed by experts to ensure the highest quality product and presentation. Because we are committed to serving our readers' needs, we welcome your feedback on how we can improve future editions of this book.

Cover design by Andrew Alcala, ABA Publishing.

Printed in the United States of America.

Library of Congress Cataloging-in-Publication Data

Selling in Your Comfort Zone: Safe and Effective Strategies for Developing New Business. Robert N. Kohn and Lawrence M. Kohn: Library of Congress Cataloging-in-Publication Data is on file.

ISBN-10: 1-60442-606-3

ISBN-13: 978-1-60442-606-9

17 16 15 5 4 3

Discounts are available for books ordered in bulk. Special consideration is given to state bars, CLE programs, and other bar-related organizations. Inquire at Book Publishing, American Bar Association, 321 N. Clark Street, Chicago, Illinois 60654-7598.

www.ShopABA.org

Dedication

We dedicate this book to the thousands of clients who have allowed us into their lives, sharing their goals, fears, setbacks, and successes. They have given us an opportunity to grow, learn, and improve our ability to help others.

Contents at a Glance

Contents

Chapter 2
Understand Your Reluctance to Sell   17

Chapter 3
Understand the Benefits of Selling   35

PART II
STRATEGIES THAT KEEP YOU IN YOUR COMFORT ZONE   41

Chapter 4
Develop Confidence in Your Ability to Offer Value   43

Chapter 5
Identify Targets in Your Comfort Zone   59

Chapter 6
Communicate Value to Your Targets   69

Chapter 7
Reveal Your Interest in Doing Business   81

Chapter 8
Find Comfortable Techniques for Meeting New People 87

Chapter 9
Develop Comfortable Systems to Stay in Touch   **101**

PART III
SKILL MODULES—TIPS FOR SAFE AND
EFFECTIVE SELLING STRATEGIES
115

Skill Module 1
Tips for Public Speaking: How to Overcome Your Fear of
Embarrassment and Maximize Your Success
117

About the Authors

The authors, Robert and Lawrence Kohn, are brothers. Since 1985, they have been providing marketing and sales consulting services to lawyers, accountants, architects, doctors, consultants, and business executives who are uncomfortable with selling.

The Kohn Brothers are pioneers in a technique that is known as executive coaching. As of the initial publication of this book, they have personally conducted over 50,000 individual coaching sessions with lawyers and other professionals across the country, and hundreds of seminars, workshops, and classes. They have published dozens of articles on the subject of marketing.

This was not a business that was created by design. Their experience in business extends back to their family's finance business. They were third-generation lenders. Their grandfather, Hyman Kohn, was also a business pioneer. He started the first automobile finance company in Chicago in 1918. The company grew and diversified into the 1930s when their father, Le Roy Kohn, became president. Their father built the company further until it became traded on the American Stock Exchange. In the 1970s, the family business was sold. The two brothers and their father started a privately-owned finance company. However, after their father's retirement, they decided, as have many third-generation family business owners, they wanted to do something different with their lives.

After many years of trial and error, including a business radio show for three years, and many experiments with different services, their current business evolved.

Their unique perspectives about selling form the basis of this book. Lawrence Kohn, an extrovert, has always loved and excelled in selling. Robert Kohn, who is more introverted, has struggled with every obstacle described in this book.

Their differences and their ability to work together to debate the issues, engage in deep introspection, and test their findings in the real world have allowed them to create a truly unique and thoughtful body of work.

Robert and Lawrence Kohn may be reached at (310) 652-1442 or **www.kohncommunications.com**.

Introduction

Is This Book for You?

If you are uncomfortable with selling but acknowledge the need to improve your selling skills, this book is for you! Of course, there are many books on selling. But, unlike other books, *this* book is primarily concerned with helping you overcome your *discomfort* with selling. There is no value in learning about selling skills if you are convinced that the things you have to do to be successful are contrary to your personality, your capability, or your moral code. Our intention is to change the way you think about selling and to help you achieve a fundamental shift in your attitudes and behavior.

This book teaches you how to sell by building quality relationships. It helps you build confidence in your ability to provide value to your clients, confidence in the quality of individuals with whom you plan to interact, and confidence that you are using appropriate communication techniques. This book helps you communicate the necessary information so that prospects can make an informed decision about hiring you. This will increase the likelihood of meeting their expectations.

Bear in mind that some professions have restrictions concerning selling. Make sure that you are aware of and comply with the rules of conduct of your profession, which for lawyers includes the ABA Model Rules of Professional Conduct.

Misconceptions and Negative Experiences

There are many preconceived notions about selling. And, chances are, you have had some distasteful experiences to reinforce your beliefs. These beliefs and experiences are deeply entrenched and can make you skeptical about your ability to sell in ways that are appropriate and effective.

Our Goals

This book sets out to prove that selling can be done effectively and *comfortably.* We are not interested in pushing you outside of your comfort zone. Our years of coaching professionals nationwide have taught us that there is no point in trying to force you to do something that you don't want to do, or believe that you can't do. We are interested in motivating you to take action. To do this, it helps to identify strategies and tasks that you are comfortable doing. It is difficult to get people to step outside of their comfort zones. Fortunately, you don't have to.

What You Will Achieve

The information in the following pages is the culmination of our many years of experience in working with highly educated, skeptical professionals. We believe that it will dramatically impact your ability to sell *and* your life. Selling is important because it will bring you greater income, security, power, new friends, intellectual stimulation, emotional fulfillment, better clients, more freedom, and fun!

Our Approach

This book is divided into three parts. Part One defines the comfort zone, and explains your reasons for your discomfort, and the risks and rewards of selling. Part Two discusses *11 strategies* to help you stay in your comfort zone. Part Three provides *eight skill modules* that will help you feel more comfortable with the selling process. These modules provide 106 tips designed to make selling safe and effective. Throughout the book, we provide *text boxes with key ideas* and *comfort zone tasks* that we recommend you experiment with.

The Table of Obstacles and Solutions

We have created the following table (see page 3) to help you quickly find solutions to obstacles you are facing. Review the bullet-point solutions, and read the parts of the book that deal with your specific areas of interest.

Conclusion

We have labored hard in creating this book. It is the result of over five years of intense thought, observation, feedback, discussion, and writing. We believe that we have touched upon some universal truths about the reasons for discomfort with selling. We are proud to present what we believe is a *comprehensive* and *practical* guide for overcoming your discomfort. We hope that you find this book to be useful and interesting.

Table of Obstacles and Solutions

This table is a quick reference to help you sell in your comfort zone by over-coming specific obstacles to selling. We provide bullet points for each solution and the location of a more in-depth discussion in the book.

Obstacles to selling	Solutions
1. Indifference	• Be aware of the benefits of selling, 35–40
2. Lack of time	• Use your time wisely, 10 • Focus on quality targets, 60–61 • Improve your systems for staying in touch, 101–114 • Improve time management skills, 171–178 • Improve delegation skills, 174–178
3. Cultural stereotypes about selling	• Don't assume that all salespeople fit the stereotype of a sales-person, 21–23 • Be aware that what makes selling good or bad is how it is done, 22
4. The risk of rejection	• Develop pride in the value you offer, 43–58 • Find targets with the potential to lead to new business, 60–61 • Identify people you like, 61–62 • Communicate value to your targets, 69–80 • Find safe environments for meeting new people, 89–99 • Overcome your fear of public speaking, 117–123 • Find safe and effective techniques for working a room, 163–166
5. The fear of failure	• Develop confidence that you are using your time wisely, 10–11 • Don't allow your fear of failure to stop you from looking for ideas that can succeed, 23–24 • Choose tasks that are achievable, 179–188
6. The belief that you are too old to learn new skills	• Know that if you are intelligent and motivated, you can improve at any age, 24
7. The misconception that selling must be abusive	• Know that selling doesn't have to be abusive, 24 • Develop pride in the value you offer, 43–58 • Develop techniques for communicating value, 69–80 • Develop comfortable systems to stay in touch, 101–114
8. The belief that you must emulate the sales styles of other people	• Find your comfort zone, 11–12 • Identify strategies that are safe, 69–80
9. The belief that selling is unethical	• Be honest and accurate, 25 • Develop strategies that communicate value, 69–80 • Learn how to reveal your interest in doing business, 81–86
10. The misconception that selling is demeaning	• Know that sophisticated, highly educated and successful professionals view selling as an important and enjoyable activity, 25–26 • Appreciate that selling can be intellectually gratifying, 40
11. The fear of being perceived as needy	• Know that to the outside world, you can be extremely talented and successful and still want to build your business, 26
12. The belief that selling makes you appear greedy	• Develop confidence in the value you offer—As long as you offer a good deal, there is nothing immoral about making money, 26, 43–58
13. The fear of boasting or bragging	• Give value-in-advance, 71–74 • Develop dialogue that accurately communicates the value you offer, 78–80

Obstacles to selling	Solutions
14. Shyness	• Understand that shyness is situational, 27 • Develop confidence in the value you offer, 43–58 • Identify targets you like, 61–62 • Develop confidence in your communication skills, 69–80 • Find selling environments that make you feel safe, 91–96
15. The myth of introversion	• Know that you don't need to change your personality, 28 • Understand the importance of selling, 35–40 • Identify targets you like, 61–62 • Identify selling activities that you enjoy, 75–76
16. The misconception of having to be best friends	• Understand the distinction between allies and friends, 28–29 • Explain your reasons for socializing, 85–86
17. The risk of misinterpretation	• Accurately reveal your interest in doing business, 81–86
18. The obstacle of not liking your business contacts	• Strive to do business with people you like, 61–62 • Identify environments for meeting quality targets, 88–99
19. The feeling of being insincere	• Select techniques that reveal your interest in doing business, 81–86
20. The risk of appearing superficial	• Talk about issues that are meaningful to your targets, 69–80, 165
21. The obstacle of reciprocation	• Know that you don't have to reciprocate by referring clients—You can reciprocate by providing other value, 30, 71–74
22. Being new to your profession (Limited experience) (Limited contacts)	• Sell your team, 31 • Know that you probably know more people than you realize, 62–65 • Build your credibility, 117–143
23. The feeling of impatience	• View selling as a long-term process, 101 • Create realistic standards of success, 179–188
24. The belief that you have started selling too late	• Appreciate that you already have many of the skills necessary to be successful in selling so you won't look like a beginner, 28
25. The belief that selling is boring	• Do things you enjoy and that are fulfilling, 75–76
26. Not liking your job	• Consider changing jobs or professions, 33
27. Lack of support for selling	• Learn how to lobby for your ideas, 33–34 • Invest in your own selling effort because the more successful you are, the more power you will have, 37
28. The force of inertia	• Take small steps and acknowledge every success that you achieve, 179–189 • Document the names of your quality contacts, 103

Obstacles and Benefits

Hope for the Reluctant

1

Hate to sell?
No need to moan
Just sell within
Your comfort zone

THE PURPOSE OF THIS BOOK is to help you overcome your discomfort with selling. We call our approach, "selling in your comfort zone."

What stops you from selling is not simply a lack of *knowledge* about selling. Bookstores are filled with books on the subject. You can buy videos and hire consultants. Unfortunately, learning *about* selling won't help you as long as the *idea* of selling remains distasteful.

It is easy to avoid doing things that you don't like, even when you recognize their benefits. For example, if you are afraid of the dentist's drill, then you may postpone going to the dentist. If you don't like physical exercise, then you might avoid going to the gym. If you don't like selling, then you'll avoid that as well.

We have had clients who have gone to great lengths to avoid selling. They'd come up with one excuse after another. One of our clients threatened to quit his job if his partners persisted in pressing him to sell. Pushing him to sell without addressing his underlying discomfort merely strengthened his resistance.

This book would be a waste of time if it simply gave you the tools for how to sell. It would be just one more sales book in an ocean of self-help books.

Our goal is to inspire you to take action. To do this, we want you to find ways of feeling comfortable with selling, and even to enjoy it. The more comfortable you feel, the more willing you will be to take action.

> ▼
>
> As long as you are uncomfortable with selling, you'll find reasons to procrastinate

Your Reasons for Reluctance

Discomfort with selling is common. The mere *mention* of the word "selling" can elicit images of sleazy, pushy, manipulative, and insincere salespeople harassing you on the telephone or hounding you around the car dealership. It can evoke feelings of neediness and rejection.

You may have an image of a salesperson as someone who is outgoing, someone who loves telling jokes, or who thrives in the limelight. You may not think of yourself as that person. Rather, you may feel shy or introverted.

Maybe you have had some bad experiences with selling. Perhaps you have been served by sales people who tried to sell you something you didn't want. Or, maybe at some point in your life you tried selling something to others and found the experience to be unpleasant.

Maybe you have developed the belief that selling shouldn't even be necessary – that you should be able to generate clients without it or that it is unprofessional. Maybe you have been able to rely on your partners or co-workers to generate clients for you. In fact, you may have been so busy doing the work that it didn't seem possible to take on more.

These are only a handful of the potential reasons for your discomfort with selling. We describe 28 obstacles to selling in Chapter 2. But for now, suffice it to say that you are facing some powerful obstacles, any *one* of which could undermine your willingness to sell.

Awakening to the Importance of Selling

One might ask, if you are so uncomfortable with selling, why bother? The answer is that something has changed your perspective. Maybe you no longer wish to be dependent on your partners or co-workers to feed you with work. Maybe you see selling as a pathway to more money or more authority in your organization. Maybe the economy has taken a turn for the worse and now there is more competition pursuing fewer clients. Maybe you have decided to start your *own* practice or business. While in the past, doing good work seemed sufficient, you have now awakened to the realization that learning how to sell would be beneficial.

But, you are blocked. You don't know where to begin or how to make the transition from *technician* to *business developer*.

Selling Doesn't Have to Be Uncomfortable

If you genuinely want to learn how to sell, you must find ways of doing it that feel comfortable. One of the principle ways that our approach differs from that of others is that we don't push you to do something that you don't want to do. If you are uncomfortable with a particular selling strategy, then we say, "_Don't_ do it!"

This doesn't mean give up. Instead, look for alternative strategies that keep you in your comfort zone.

A Case in Point

One of our clients was reluctant to sell because in his mind, selling meant violating his moral code of appropriate behavior. He believed that it positioned him negatively in his clients' minds. He was skeptical about the effectiveness of selling, and said that his past efforts had never generated any business.

When we asked him to define what he meant by selling, he said that selling meant going to networking events where he had to walk up to complete strangers, give them his business cards, and try to persuade them to hire him. He had gone to several such networking events and found the experiences to be both repugnant and a waste of time. He concluded that selling was not for him and he dismissed anyone's efforts to convince him to the contrary.

Rather than try and convince him to do something that he refused to do, our advice was:

> "Don't go to networking events. In fact, don't do anything that takes you out of your comfort zone. There are other things you can do to sell your services that do not require leaving your comfort zone."

Over the next several months, we helped him redefine selling and to identify strategies that felt comfortable. We have included these strategies in this book. Once he understood that he could sell in his comfort zone, he began to look at selling in a new way. He learned to embrace it. And, he began to experience great success.

▼

If a strategy is uncomfortable, don't do it.

What Is the Comfort Zone?

There are two components of selling in your comfort zone: _safety_ and _effectiveness_.

Safety

By safety, we mean that your sales techniques must be appropriate for your personality, your beliefs, your values, your interests, and your level of experience with selling. Your techniques must minimize the risk of feeling embarrassed. Furthermore, you must believe that *other* people will perceive your selling behavior as appropriate.

Effectiveness

By effectiveness, we mean that you must be optimistic that you are using your time and money wisely. You must feel confident that your efforts will realistically lead to new business.

The Comfort Quadrant

The standards for what is safe and effective are different for each person. You must discover what is right for you. To help you determine whether or not an activity falls inside your comfort zone, you can chart it on the following grid.

In Figure 1, we provide a grid with two perpendicular axes. The vertical axis is the "safety" axis. The horizontal axis is the "effectiveness" axis. The upper right quadrant formed by the two axes is called the ***comfort***

Figure 1

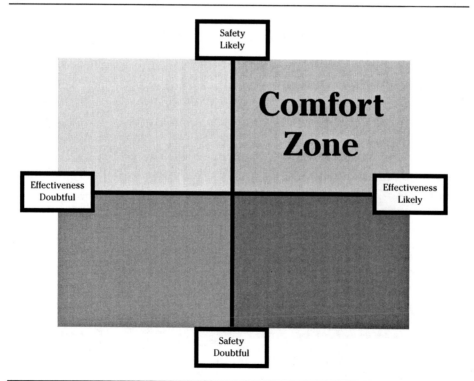

quadrant. For a particular activity to be in your comfort zone, it must give you a high expectation of both safety and effectiveness.

Find Your Comfort Zone

Here are some examples of how selling activities can fall into the four different quadrants.

Safety Likely, Effectiveness Likely (The Comfort Quadrant)

If you enjoy a particular activity and believe that it is likely to result in new business, then that activity falls into this quadrant. For example, some people feel very comfortable with socializing. They enjoy lunches and dinners with clients and other business contacts. They also say that they get business from socializing. For these people, socializing is in their comfort zone. It provides both a high expectation of safety and effectiveness.

Safety Doubtful, Effectiveness Likely

However, you may not enjoy socializing with clients and business contacts. You may acknowledge that socializing might be effective in developing new business, but it feels awkward or manipulative. So, for you, socializing would fall into the lower-right quadrant: Effectiveness likely, safety doubtful.

Safety Likely, Effectiveness Doubtful

You may enjoy social activities like taking clients to dinners and ballgames. But, you may not believe that these activities will help you generate any business. So, these activities would be placed in the upper-left quadrant: Safety likely, effectiveness doubtful.

Safety Doubtful, Effectiveness Doubtful

Tasks that have a low expectation of both safety and effectiveness fall into this category. If you don't like speaking, writing, or socializing, and don't have any faith in the value of these activities, then they will be in the lower-left quadrant.

The Comfort Zone Is Dynamic

This book is designed to help you identify tasks that are within the comfort quadrant—safety likely, effectiveness likely—however limited that may currently be. Fortunately, your beliefs about what is safe and effective can change. You can learn to increase your expectations of safety and effectiveness.

Increase Your Level of Safety

Throughout this book, we give examples of how to increase your expectation of safety with selling activities, even things you currently don't imagine doing. For example, there are practical ways to increase your comfort with business socializing, public speaking, networking, and other sales-related activities.

Increase Your Level of Effectiveness

You can also overcome your skepticism about the value of selling activities. We show you how to improve your targeting skills and your ability to communicate value. These skills will greatly improve your chances of success.

Slow and Steady Wins the Race

Overcoming your discomfort will most likely be a gradual process. Begin by identifying small, safe tasks that get you started. Look for tasks that are fun and stimulating. As you gain practice and experience success, your level of safety and effectiveness will increase. Upon finishing this book, we believe that what feels uncomfortable to you now will seem perfectly natural and comfortable.

Don't Be Too Quick to Give Up

Because this will be a gradual process, you must develop a willingness to continue searching for tasks in your comfort zone. Too many people make a cursory effort at sales. They have an image in their minds of what it means to sell, and they give up without out any further thought. Their beliefs and experiences with selling make them skeptical that it can be done both safely and effectively. Don't allow your skepticism to prevent you from looking for other available options.

> Never let what you *can't* do stop you from looking for what you *can* do.

Consistent, Constructive Attention

The key to your success in selling is a philosophy that we call "consistent, constructive attention." This means staying focused on selling and consistently looking for safe and effective ideas.

> Attention → Awareness → Motivation → Action → Success

We have identified a formula for success we call AAMAS, which is an acronym for:

Attention → Awareness → Motivation → Action → Success.

This formula relates to selling as follows: The more consistent and constructive attention you apply to your selling effort, the more ideas you become aware of—ideas for meeting new people and for communicating with the people you have already met. The more ideas you become aware of, the more motivated you will feel to take action. The more action you take, the more success you are likely to enjoy.

The Willingness to Pay Attention

People who are good at selling were not born with some magical talent or personality. There is no such thing as a "selling gene." Rather, they think about selling all of the time, often because they enjoy it. If one strategy fails, they look for others. They make selling a fundamental focus. They consistently and constructively pay attention to selling.

> There is no such thing as a selling gene.

You can see this principle illustrated in your own life. Think of some challenging activity that you enjoy. Consider how much you think about it.

For example, a lot of people we know enjoy the game of golf. They enjoy everything about it. They love getting out into the fresh air. They love the sensation of swinging and hitting the ball. They love hearing the unmistakable sound of the ball dropping into the cup. They enjoy the socializing that takes place during and after the game. And, because they love it so much, they look for opportunities to play. They seek out other people who enjoy the game.

If they make a few bad shots, they don't give up. They don't say, "Well, I missed that shot. I guess I'll quit." No, of course not. They practice more. They take lessons. They read books and watch videos. They buy new clubs.

People pay attention to things they enjoy and make time for them. By doing so, they are more likely to improve. This is what happens with selling. Once you identify something you enjoy about selling, you'll give it more attention and your skills will improve.

Some people might think this approach is overly coddling. Our culture encourages a more stoic attitude. If you know that you need to sell, just do it. Be tough. If you are uncomfortable with selling, get over it. Stop whining. No pain, no gain. That's the conventional wisdom.

The problem with this stoic mindset is that while it sounds good, it thwarts action. You may appreciate the concept, "No pain, no gain." But, you are more likely to live by the philosophy: "Fear pain, Abstain." If you push yourself to do something that you find inherently distasteful, you either

> You are more likely to live by the philosophy, "Fear pain, abstain."

are not going to stick with it long enough to yield results, or you won't even give it a try. Any approach that doesn't help you overcome your discomfort is a prescription for failure.

We're not saying that selling is easy. Just like anything that is worthwhile, it is hard work. You have to think, do research, plan, practice, and be persistent. But, it doesn't have to be distasteful. You can sell in your comfort zone.

The Structure of This Book

This book is divided into three main parts. In Part I, we help you understand the reasons for your discomfort, and the benefits for overcoming your obstacles.

Part II provides the following 11 strategies that will help you to stay in your comfort zone:

1. Develop confidence in your ability to offer value
2. Identify targets with the potential to lead to new business
3. Identify targets you like
4. Give "value-in-advance"
5. Develop dialogue that communicates value
6. Develop documents that communicate value
7. Reveal your interest in doing business
8. Encourage introductions from people you know
9. Get involved in organizations
10. Develop your contact database
11. Improve your relationship development skills

Part III provides the following 8 skill modules containing tips on implementing specific selling skills in safe and effective ways:

1. Tips for public speaking; how to overcome your fear of embarrassment and maximize your success
2. Tips for conducting effective seminars
3. Tips for effective and affordable public relations
4. Tips for documenting the value that you offer
5. Tips for client satisfaction surveys
6. Tips for comfortably working a room
7. Tips for time management
8. Tips for creating an achievable strategic plan

How to Use This Book

First, create a file. As you read the book, write down concepts that are meaningful to you on a separate sheet of paper and keep them in the file. Changing the way you think about selling can be a long-term process. Reading this book will introduce you to the concepts, but the changes that are necessary won't happen overnight. Capturing key concepts and then re-reading them in your own handwriting will help you develop a new awareness.

Review the table of obstacles and solutions on page 3. Look for the obstacles that apply to you and study the solutions.

Once you have identified some comfortable strategies, commit to implement some tasks. A task may be to do some research or some thinking. Or, it may be to experiment with a specific communication technique that we describe.

After completing a task, review the sections of the book that deal with that task. Decide where it belongs on the comfort grid. If it still remains in the comfort quadrant, then keep working at it. Continue committing to additional small steps.

If we were personally instructing you, we would reinforce our lessons over and over until they become a habit. Since we are not physically present to instruct you, you have to be your own coach. Give yourself assignments from the book and continually review the lessons. This process of identifying strategies, evaluating your comfort level, committing to implement, and then reviewing your progress, will lead to a new awareness and comfort with selling. It will open your eyes to a new world of possibilities.

Conclusion

If you have never been comfortable with selling, it may be hard to imagine that it is possible to overcome your discomfort. Nevertheless, we have helped thousands of individuals overcome their reluctance and achieve success.

By studying the principles described in this book, you too can learn how to sell in your comfort zone. It is an exciting, life-changing experience.

So, let's get started!

Understand Your Reluctance to Sell

2

When building your muscles, no pain means no gain,
But pain when you're selling might make you refrain.
So look for the reasons for why you resist,
And you'll find solutions to help you persist.

THE FIRST STEP in overcoming your discomfort with selling is to become aware of your thoughts about selling. Pay attention to your "internal voice," which is your stream of consciousness. Everyone has an internal voice. You may not be aware of it all of the time, but it is always with you and it profoundly influences your feelings and actions.

Notice Your Negative Voice

If you are uncomfortable with selling, then your internal voice becomes your "negative voice." You develop a pattern of dwelling on the reasons why you shouldn't sell.

Your negative voice tends to be habitual and automatic. It's like a knee-jerk reaction. Whenever you imagine yourself doing some selling-oriented activity, your negative voice argues, "I can't do that," or "I don't want to do that." You literally talk yourself out of selling.

A Case of the "Yeah, buts"

When we discuss selling with clients and prospects who have made up their minds not to sell, the pattern of focusing on the negative is apparent. We were talking with a managing partner in an accounting firm who was resistant to selling. Even though he wanted to sell more, he came up with one excuse after another why he couldn't. Our conversation went like this:

> Partner: "I love selling. I would do more of it but I'm busy. There just isn't enough time in the day to do my work *and* sell."

> Kohn: "Maybe you could free up time by delegating? There must be many tasks that you could delegate to other people in your firm."

> Partner: "Yeah, but by the time I explain something to someone, I could do it myself. Besides, there is nobody here who can do my job as well as I do it."

> Kohn: "Surely, there are smart people here. Maybe they don't do everything the way you do it. But they could learn."

> Partner: "Yeah, but my clients ask for me. They would be upset if I delegated their assignments to anyone else."

> Kohn: "You could explain to your clients that they would be better served having someone who is qualified but at a lower billing rate do the work. It would save them money. And, you could stay involved to make sure that your clients are satisfied."

> Partner: "Yeah, but I'm tired of being the only one in this firm who generates business. It is time that others take on the responsibility. I bring in most of the work and I am fed up with how other people don't do any selling."

> Kohn: "We certainly appreciate that others must learn to sell and we're going to help them. But, it could take a long time for them to see results. Since you already have quality relationships with clients and referral sources, you'll have quicker results if you increase your selling effort. Besides, it is hard to inspire others to do something that you're unwilling to do."

> Partner: Yeah, but I need to spend more time with my family. I have a wife and two daughters and they demand my time. I can't do everything and still spend time with my family."

> Kohn: "You don't have to sacrifice family time. You could contact people over the phone during the day. You could take your clients and referral sources to lunch."

> Partner: "Yeah, but the kind of selling I do requires that I attend meetings in the evenings when my family wants me to be with them."

Kohn: "Well, you don't have to take every evening off. You could find meetings that only require your time once or twice a month. We're suggesting that you increase your selling effort a little. It doesn't have to consume your life."

Partner: "Yeah, but my daughters would still be upset, even with only once or twice a month."

Kohn: "Well, you could explain to your daughters that in the long-run your ability to generate more revenue would ultimately give them a better life and free up more time in the future."

Partner: "Yeah, but you don't know my daughters!"

This partner had an unrelenting case of the "Yeah-buts." His pattern was to defend his lack of selling. He had made up his mind that he couldn't sell. Every time we offered a solution to an obstacle, he was quick to find another reason to support his decision not to sell. Of course, each of his reasons had some validity. The important concept to note is the knee-jerk response to defend his position rather than figure out how to solve the problem.

> ▼
> A "Yeah-but" response may indicate an anti-selling sentiment.

Your Negative Voice Is Deeply Entrenched

Your negative voice has probably been with you for a long time. Many of our clients have told us that they have had negative experiences with selling since childhood. One of our clients vividly remembers the distasteful experience of having to sell raffle tickets for his grammar school. And, although he is now grown, he is still haunted by that negative experience.

Because your negative voice is so deeply entrenched, you may take it for granted. It feels like a friend. It appears to be protecting you against embarrassment and failure.

But, the fact is that in many cases, your negative voice is a false friend. It stops you from looking for safe and effective strategies to generate new business. For example, one individual we know was absolutely resolute in his belief that he shouldn't ask his clients for additional work. Even though he had never raised the issue with any of his clients, he was convinced that they would be offended if he brought it up. In his mind, his untested belief had become fact.

Ultimately, we helped him find a comfortable way of raising the issue with one of his clients and it was received positively. We taught him how to reveal his interest in doing business. It is a technique that many of our clients find safe and effective. We describe it in Chapter 7. Once our client learned that he could comfortably reveal his interest in doing business, it shattered his old prejudice and opened a door of opportunities. But, he had to experience first-hand that his anti-selling sentiment, which he had taken for granted for his entire career, was invalid.

Challenge Your Negative Voice

We are not saying that your negative voice is *always* wrong. Sometimes your anti-selling beliefs are valid. For example, there may be a risk of being overly pushy with some of your prospects. If you follow up with a prospect incessantly, without offering value, there is the possibility of harming a relationship. So, you want acknowledge your negative voice.

But often, your negative voice is prejudiced and incorrect. You jump to conclusions that may be based on unclear and erroneous assumptions. You focus only on the negative, and ignore all of the safe and effective things that you *could* be doing.

So, avoid the knee-jerk reaction of accepting your negative voice as fact. Instead, develop the habit of challenging your negative voice. When you do, you will probably find that many of your long-held convictions about selling are untrue.

Develop a Proactive Selling Attitude

We have had many clients, who were extremely reluctant to sell. Many of them told us that a meeting with us was worse than a trip to the dentist. Every idea that we suggested would be instantly shot down. But, as we helped them become aware of their anti-selling sentiments and find ways to comfortably overcome them, their attitudes became more positive. They became more accepting of selling ideas and more enthusiastic about business development. They developed a proactive selling attitude.

A wonderful thing happens when you develop a proactive selling attitude. You begin to notice selling opportunities that you didn't realize existed. Selling opportunities are often all around you. You may know people who can help you meet quality contacts. There are organizations that may be fun for you to join that could also bring you into contact with quality contacts.

> Your negative voice blinds you to the opportunities around you.

As you read this book, you will see that there are many safe and effective ways to sell. When you consistently and constructively think about ways to improve your selling, you will alter your pattern of automatic negative thinking, and open your mind to solutions.

28 Reasons for Your Reluctance to Sell

To help you become aware of your negative voice, we have compiled a list of 28 common obstacles to selling. We have assembled this list from the thousands of coaching sessions and seminars we have conducted across the country. In this section, we explain and challenge each obstacle.

We know that the list of obstacles is long. But, we recommend that you review them all. Your ability to sell in your comfort zone is dependent upon your understanding the obstacles that stand in your way. The more quickly you notice your negative voice, the faster you will be able to evaluate it, and focus on finding safe and effective ways to sell.

1. Indifference to selling:

"I don't think selling is important."

Indifference toward selling is one of the most challenging obstacles. If you don't see the need, you won't care about it enough to give it your attention. In Chapter 3, we delve into the benefits of selling. After you finish reading the next chapter, you will see that indifference is a luxury you can't afford.

2. Lack of time:

"I am too busy to sell."

Almost all of our clients are busy. They have demanding schedules. They have personal lives outside of work. Many of our clients say they are so busy that they don't have time to do the work on their desks, much less look for more.

And, in fact, there probably will be times when you *are* too busy to sell. If this is the case, you may have to rearrange your schedule, or learn how to delegate tasks to make time for selling. We provide tips for time management and delegation in Skill Module 8. But often, the belief that you are too busy is a smokescreen for the underlying truth that you are uncomfortable with selling. Once you learn how to sell in your comfort zone, you will find, as many of our clients have, that there usually *is* time for selling.

3. Cultural stereotypes:

"I think selling is sleazy."

Another common reason for the reluctance to sell is the image of the salesperson as portrayed in our culture. The salesperson is often represented as a pariah—someone who is pushy, manipulative, and insincere. You don't have to look very far to find these stereotypes.

Webster's Definition of Selling

If you look in Webster's Dictionary, you'll see many negative definitions of selling such as: "To give up in return for something else especially foolishly or dishonorably; to give into the power of another (as in selling your soul to the Devil); to dispose of or manage for profit instead of in accordance with conscience, justice, or duty; to impose on or cheat; to betray."[1]

Our Definition of Selling

We believe that selling is neutral. It is neither good nor bad. We define selling as "communicating with the intent to conduct business." What makes selling good or bad is how it's done. In this book, we teach honorable techniques for selling that will make you feel proud of who you are, proud of what you are offering, and proud of how you interact with others.

> ▼
> What makes selling good or bad is how it is done.

The Image Portrayed in Literature, Movies, and Stage

Literature, movies, and stage abound with sleazy images of salespeople. In the American literature classic, *Death of a Salesman*, the main character Willie Loman is depicted as a pathetic loser. His very name speaks of lowness. In the play and movie *Glengarry Glen Ross*, salespeople are portrayed as ruthless, backstabbing liars.

In a scene from the movie, *Tin Men*, a group of aluminum siding salesmen are describing the dishonest sales techniques they use. The main character gives an example of how to win a prospect's trust. He explains:

> "If you want to win a guy's confidence, here's a good thing to try. You start off with a $5.00 bill in your hand which you take out before he's seen it. You're sitting in the living room and you're talking. And, when he's not looking you drop it on the floor. When he turns around you say, 'Oh, a five-dollar bill. You must have dropped it.' At which point, one of two things will happen. Either he'll say it's not his, and you say, "Well it's not mine, sir. It must be yours.' Or, he'll take it. In either case, he thinks you're an incredibly honest guy and you're in."

In the 1957 Broadway production, *The Music Man*, Professor Harold Hill, a slick, traveling salesman, sells musical instruments and uniforms to the townspeople. He convinces them that he is going to form a marching band for their children. He promotes his own scientific technique called

---

[1]*Merriam-Webster's Collegiate Dictionary*, Eleventh Edition, 2003.

"The Think System," in which you think the notes and are able to play them. Of course, there never is a band. Professor Hill leaves each town just before the people figure out they've been swindled.

These examples from literature, movies, and stage demonstrate how our culture stereotypes salespeople. It is easy to buy into the image. The writers are talented and the actors bring credibility to their roles. We all have had enough bad experiences with sales people that make us quick to agree with these stereotypes.

But, it is important that you stop assuming that all salespeople are disreputable. While it is true that, as in all professions, there are sleazy individuals; it doesn't mean that all salespeople are sleazy. Nor does it mean that all sales techniques are inappropriate.

The fact is that there are high-quality salespeople who are honest, knowledgeable, and caring. This book will prove that effective selling can be done honorably.

4. The risk of rejection:

"I am afraid of being turned down."

One of the most difficult obstacles to overcome is the fear of rejection. The fear of rejection is essentially the fear of being judged harshly. Nobody is comfortable with the idea of being judged harshly. The fear of being rejected in sales is frequently compared to the experience of being turned down for a date or not being asked to dance at the high school ball.

Of course, in business, the fear of rejection is usually not personal. There is a big difference between someone not being interested in using your services and not liking *you*. People may like you and still not want or be able to hire you. Nonetheless, it feels like personal rejection.

Selling is a relationship-based process. There is no way of getting around it. So, one of the requirements of selling in your comfort zone involves learning how to minimize your fear of rejection. As you read through the chapters in this book, you will find many practical techniques for doing this.

5. The risk of failure:

"Selling has never worked for me."

In selling, as with most worthwhile endeavors, you can anticipate some failure. You may have had some failures in the past. And, ideas for future action may not be readily apparent. But, that doesn't mean that they don't exist. It is important not to allow your fear of failure to prevent you from looking for ideas that could work.

Throughout this book, we provide dozens of proven techniques that will help you increase your confidence in having success. Not everything we mention may be right for your situation. But, don't give yourself permission to give up. There are always comfortable strategies you can try.

6. The belief that you are too old to learn new skills:

"You can't teach an old dog, new tricks."

This is a common belief, but it just isn't true. If you are intelligent and motivated, you can improve at any age.

7. The misconception that selling must be abusive:

"I don't want to be a pest."

A common misconception is the belief that selling is inherently annoying, manipulative, and deceitful. You may believe that selling requires you to be pushy. You may believe that you have to exaggerate the value that you offer or use manipulative techniques to convince others to retain your services.

Experiences with Abusive Salespeople

This misconception often stems from experiences with poorly trained sales representatives who are not focused on the well-being of their prospects. For example, you have probably gotten aggravating phone calls from telemarketers who interrupt you when you are busy and who try to sell you things that you don't want.

Often, these telemarketers begin their calls with blatant lies such as, "This is not a telemarketing call." Or they ask, "How are you today?" when you know they don't care. If you associate selling with inconsiderate, poorly trained salespeople, it is understandable why you would cringe at the thought of selling.

Fortunately, you don't have to be abusive. The key to selling in your comfort zone is to find techniques for accurately communicating the value that you offer and appropriately revealing your interest in doing business.

Lack of Confidence in the Value That You Offer

The misconception that selling is abusive may also come from having a lack of confidence in the value that you offer. A lot of professionals and business people are not fully convinced that they offer a good deal. A lot of people believe that they may be overcharging their clients, or that their competitors offer a better deal.

> Selling in your comfort zone requires pride in the value you offer, and pride in your communication techniques.

If you are not proud of the value you offer, then obviously you will feel that you are abusing people. You can overcome this obstacle by developing greater confidence in your ability offer value. We discuss this at great length in Chapter 4.

8. The belief that you must emulate other people's sales styles:

"I don't like asking for business."

Another reason for reluctance may be the belief that you have to emulate the sales styles of people you have observed. Perhaps you have been turned off by people who you felt were overly aggressive in their sales style. We had a client who was offended by the way his partner would say to his prospects, "Why aren't you sending me your business?" At networking functions, his partner would walk up to complete strangers and say, "Here is my business card. Call me." Our client recoiled at the idea of selling because in his mind, selling meant emulating his partner's style.

Another professional we were hired to assist dodged our phone calls for over three months because she was so skeptical about her ability to sell in a manner that felt appropriate. When we finally reached her, it was clear that she possessed many prejudices about selling. For example, she said, "All of the rainmakers I know are bold and outspoken. I am not so bold and outspoken. I have trouble asking for the business."

Fortunately, you don't have to emulate the styles of other people. Throughout this book, we will show you techniques for selling that are appropriate for your values and personality.

9. The belief that selling is unethical:

"My profession has rules that restrict selling."

Many professions have rules of conduct that restrict how you can sell. Clearly, you need to be aware of your profession's ethical rules. But, be careful not to categorically dismiss the idea that you can find ethical ways of selling. The professional codes that restrict selling are designed to protect the consumer against fraud and misrepresentation. As long as you are honorable and accurate, you can find ways of selling that meet the guidelines of your profession.

10. The misconception that selling is demeaning:

"Selling is for dummies."

Another major obstacle to selling is the common belief that selling is demeaning. There is the perception that selling is for uneducated people with limited skills. After all, it doesn't require any degrees or licensing.

But, selling doesn't have to be demeaning. We regularly work with sophisticated, highly educated, successful professionals and business people who see selling as an enjoyable and important part of their lives. They are comfortable with selling because they are proud of both what they offer and the methods they use to interact with people.

11. The fear of being perceived as needy:

"People will think I'm a loser."

There is a common misconception that selling means that you don't have enough business to support yourself. One of our clients once stated, "Selling makes me feel like a loser."

Selling doesn't mean that you are needy. Selling simply means that you want to offer your products or services to the market place. From the perspective of the outside world, you can be extremely talented and successful and still want to build your business.

12. The belief that selling makes you appear greedy:

"People will think I only care about money."

A lot of people are uncomfortable with selling because they are taught that the client's well-being should come first. This is true. But, the fact is that one of the main reasons you are in business is to earn a living. There is nothing greedy about selling, as long as you offer a good deal. We define a good deal as a ratio of benefits to cost in which the benefits you offer are equal to or exceed the amount you charge. The more benefits you offer, the more comfortable you will feel that you offer a good deal. We discuss this at great length in Chapter 4.

13. The fear of boasting or bragging:

"I don't like bragging about myself."

Many clients have told us that they were reared with moral standards that admonished self-aggrandizement. As a result, it feels inappropriate to promote their positive qualities.

It is true that an important aspect of selling involves revealing positive qualities. As you will see in Chapter 4, it is important to reveal qualities such as your knowledge, experience, efficiency, honesty, and loyalty. This is because people typically choose to do business with the people who they like and trust. However, this doesn't mean that you have to boast or brag.

As you will see in Chapter 6, there are many ways of safely and effectively revealing value without boasting or bragging. One example is a technique we call "value-in-advance." There are many categories of "value-in-advance," such as education, entertainment, introductions, and leadership. As you help people by giving "value-in-advance," you safely and effectively reveal a lot about your personal qualities and the value that you offer.

14. Shyness:

"I don't have a personality for selling."

Many people say that they are uncomfortable with selling because they are shy. Shyness is normal. From time to time, everybody feels shy. Shyness is an adaptive mechanism that arises in social situations in which there are risks of being judged harshly.

Unfortunately, in our American culture, shyness has a negative stigma. According to Philip G. Zimbardo, Ph.D., one of the pioneers in researching shyness, our American culture values traits such as "leadership, assertiveness, dominance, independence, and risk taking." People who are most likely to be successful are "heroes, actors, athletes, politicians, television personalities, and rock stars—people expert at calling attention to themselves: Madonna, Rosanne, and Howard Stern."[2]

The irony is that as many as half of the American population, possibly more, consider themselves to be shy. Zimbardo points out that you can overcome your feelings of shyness by improving your communication skills. We say that you can overcome your shyness by improving your ability to communicate value. The more confidence you have that your prospects appreciate the value you offer, the more comfortable you will feel in reaching out to them. A large portion of this book is devoted to helping you develop confidence in your ability to communicate value.

Shyness Is Situational

Shyness is often misunderstood as a personality trait. Actually, your level of shyness depends upon the situation you are in. You may feel shy around strangers, but absolutely comfortable when you are with people you know.

In this book, we help you to find environments for selling in which you won't feel shy. For example, in Chapter 8, we give you tips for getting involved in organizations in which you can get to know and feel comfortable with people.

▼

You can be shy and still be comfortable with selling.

---

[2]"Are you shy?," *Psychology Today Magazine*, Nov. 1995, Carducci, Zimbardo.

15. The myth of introversion:

"I am not the life of the party."

Unlike shyness, introversion *is* a personality trait. However, there is a myth about introverts. It is presumed that they can't interact well with others. The truth is that introverts can have the skills and self-esteem necessary for interacting successfully with others, but, by nature, prefer to be alone. A common theory is that introverts need solitude to recharge their creative, emotional, and intellectual energy.[3]

Selling is a social activity, so being an introvert may be an obstacle. Extroverts often have an advantage in sales because they enjoy meeting people. They seek out environments in which they are likely to come into contact with people. When they are in public, they naturally look for people who they know or opportunities to meet complete strangers because they enjoy it.

If you are an introvert, your lifestyle may not support selling. You may prefer to avoid large groups of people. And, when you *are* out in public, you may not feel inclined to interact.

While being an introvert may be an obstacle to selling, it doesn't necessarily prevent you from being comfortable with it. In fact, introverts often become exceptional salespeople. We know many individuals with introverted personalities who love to entertain, speak in front of large audiences, and take high-profile leadership roles in organizations.

For some professions, being introverted may actually provide a selling advantage. For example, you may expect someone such as a CPA, a psychologist, or a medical doctor to be introverted.

For purposes of learning how to sell, one of the most important lessons for introverts to learn is that you don't have to change your personality. You never need to tell a joke or be the life of the party. Rather, you need to feel assured that you will make time to be alone. And, when you plan time to be with others, it can be pleasant and worthwhile.

> ▼
> You never need to tell a joke or be the life of the party.

16. The misconception of having to be best friends:

"I don't want to be friends with my business contacts."

A common misunderstanding in selling is that you need to become friends with people before you try to sell them something. Many of our clients don't like the idea of having to be friends with their prospects and referral

---

[3]*Source: Understanding the Introvert*, Jo Ann Telfer, PhD, DPsych, Women's Health Centre May/June 2004 Newsletter.

sources. The fact is that you don't have to be. Rather, you need to develop what we call "business alliances."

There is a distinction between allies and friends. We define a "business ally" as someone who appreciates the value you offer and who, in turn, can offer value to you. Friendship implies more of a close personal relationship.

While it is true that you have to be "friendly" to develop business alliances, you don't need to become "friends." You can maintain a distant, professional relationship with people and still communicate how you can help each other. Much of this book is devoted to teaching you the process of building quality business alliances.

17. The risk of misinterpretation:

"I don't want people to get the wrong impression."

A lot of people are reluctant to sell because of the risk that their communication may be misconstrued as social. When you invite someone to lunch or a drink after work to discuss business, it might be mistaken for taking a personal interest. The solution is to make sure that you intentions are clear. In Chapter 7, we discuss ways of accurately revealing your intentions to do business.

18. The obstacle of not liking your business contacts:

"I don't like my clients."

Another obstacle to selling is the belief that you have to spend time with people that you are not interested in, or don't even like. We had a client who hated the idea of selling because he was extremely unhappy with the character of his clients. He saw them as pushy and demanding, and as basically disagreeable human beings. The thought of bringing in more of the same types of clients was extremely distasteful. As a result, he didn't feel at all compelled to promote his services.

We helped our client create a standard for desirable clients who shared his values and interests, who wouldn't push his ethical limits, or try to squeeze every nickel. Once he felt confident that he didn't have to pursue people that he didn't like, he felt better about reaching out to new people.

> ▼
> Always strive to find clients and referral sources that you like and respect.

Unfortunately, you may not always be able to eliminate working with undesirable people. You may have the classic problem of the "Golden Handcuffs." You are financially dependent upon clients that you don't like. One of the benefits of selling is that it gives you the opportunity to upgrade the quality of your clientele.

In Chapter 5, we provide techniques for identifying people who you like and respect. And, in Chapter 8, we provide some practical techniques for meeting these people. As you become successful in developing more desirable clients, you can enjoy the experience of terminating undesirable clients.

19. The obstacle of being insincere:

"I don't like feeling transparent."

A lot of people are reluctant to sell because they fear that their efforts to be friendly will be seen as nothing more than a veiled attempt to get business. The solution to this problem is to find the right words to convey your desire to both be friends and to have a business component in your relationship. See Chapter 7 for appropriate techniques of revealing your interest in doing business.

20. The risk of feeling superficial:

"I don't like making small talk."

A lot of people don't like selling because of the belief that you have to talk about things you really don't care about. You believe that selling is nothing more than "small talk."

The truth is that selling requires learning about important issues in the lives of your prospects and referral sources and providing helpful responses. Selling is only superficial if you avoid substance. While in some circumstances, you may need to open with less important dialogue, the more quickly you engage in meaningful issues, the better.

21. The obstacle of reciprocation:

"I don't have enough business to refer to everyone I know."

Another reason many people are reluctant to sell is the fear of having to reciprocate. There is an old saying that goes, "You scratch my back and I'll scratch yours." In selling this means that if a person refers a client to you then you must send a client to them. But, it is unrealistic to believe that you can send business to everyone who sends business to you. For example, if you get business from CPAs, you can't realistically give business to every CPA you know.

While we believe in making referrals whenever possible, there are other ways of reciprocating. As you will see in Chapters 4 and 6, you have the ability to offer different types of value. For example, you can introduce people to some of the people you know who in turn could introduce your contacts to new clients. Or, you can provide education and entertainment. Simply doing good work for the clients of your contacts may be sufficient value. There are many forms of quality reciprocation.

22. Being new to your profession:

"I am too young and inexperienced."

There are two aspects to the obstacle of being new to your profession: limited experience and limited contacts.

Limited Experience

People who are new to their professions often say that they are uncomfortable with selling because they haven't had a lot of experience in their fields. There is also the possibility that prospects will be skeptical about dealing with someone who is new and inexperienced.

In time, you will become older and more experienced. Meanwhile, one solution is to sell your team. Offer the expertise of the more experienced people in your organization. If you are a solo practitioner, consider joining networking groups that provide entrée to knowledgeable resources.

Keep in mind that if someone asks you a question for which you do not have the answer, never try to "fake it" and risk the wrong answer. It is perfectly appropriate to say, "I don't know. I will get back to you with an answer." Then, do your research and respond. This will build your knowledge and keep you connected with your prospect.

Limited Contacts

Being new to your profession may also mean that you don't have many contacts that could help you generate new business. If you are just getting started in your profession, be patient. It takes time to meet the right contacts. But, don't use this fact to justify putting off your selling effort until later. This would be a mistake. Building business relationships is a long-term process. There are a lot of things you could be doing right now to plant seeds for the future.

▼
Start selling now.
It is a mistake to wait.

You could get involved in organizations that bring you into environments where you could meet quality contacts (Chapter 8). You could also build your mailing list and develop systems for staying in touch with the people that you meet (Chapter 9). The more you focus on developing your network today, the easier and faster it will be to promote your services in the future.

23. The feeling of impatience:

"Selling takes too long."

Learning to sell can seem overwhelming. It could take many years to meet prospects and convert them into clients. Our advice is to be patient and stay focused on the selling process.

Selling Is a Process

Selling is a process that has many critical steps. The process involves identifying the right people to communicate with, building trust and rapport, and maintaining a consistent, positive presence in their lives. You have no control over many factors. Much of selling is dependent upon timing. Your prospects have to have a need for your services, the financial capacity to afford your services, and the authority to hire you. The key to success is to be engaged in the activities over which you have control such as meeting new contacts, staying in touch, and strengthening your skills.

It is unrealistic to believe that you could start with minimal contacts and sales skills and immediately bring in new clients. You shouldn't gauge your success exclusively by how much new business you generate. Of course, this is your ultimate objective. But, you will be disappointed if your only measurement of success is new business. You need to acknowledge your intermediate successes with each step in the process.

▼

Have faith in the selling process.

24. The belief that you have started selling too late:

"I am embarrassed to start selling at this time in my career."

If you have been in business or practice for many years, you may feel that you are starting too late. It may feel embarrassing for someone at your stage in life to start something new and look like a beginner.

But, the fact is that what we teach is common sense. You probably already have many of the skills necessary to be successful in selling but you haven't applied them. So, you won't look like a beginner.

25. The belief that selling is boring:

"I don't enjoy schmoozing."

A common belief about selling is that it is boring. The belief is that you have to spend time with people you don't like and do things that you don't enjoy. However, selling can be fun. We know many professionals who have built their practices around their personal interests and hobbies. One successful client we worked with built a book of clients with people who shared his love of auto racing. Another client built a base of clients with people who shared his passion for baseball.

26. Not liking your job:

"I don't enjoy my work."

If you don't like what you do for a living, it will be difficult to inspire others to use your services. Although the scope of this book doesn't include finding a new job or career, this is something you should consider if you are unhappy in your current situation.

27. Lack of support for selling:

"I am the only one in my firm who thinks this is important."

If you work in a company or a firm, you may encounter a lack of support for your selling efforts. This lack of support may come in several forms. Some firms simply ignore selling. Some firms pay lip service to it but fail to provide resources. And some firms are actually hostile toward it.

We know a lot of people who actually resent or look down on the efforts of their colleagues who sell. One of our clients in a law firm was constantly getting negative feedback for selling. Even though she was a successful business developer, her partners still were unable to grasp the value of her selling efforts. She was criticized for putting on events, taking trips to conventions, and entertaining people. She was chastised for spending the firm's money instead of billing time.

The skepticism and resentment that your colleagues may feel is reinforced by the fact that a lot of selling is fun. Sure, selling can be hard work. But, it also involves entertainment, going to nice restaurants, and visiting interesting places. Often, partners would rather have that money in their own pockets instead of dedicating it to someone else's selling activity, or to what they might consider to be an excessive boondoggle.

Even after a successful business development activity, colleagues can remain skeptical. Often, it is not clear-cut whether or not an activity was worthwhile. How do you know for example if a party was necessary? How do you know if a golf tournament resulted in new business? Even if you got new business after these activities, your colleagues might argue that the people who attended and hired you would have hired you anyway.

It is important that you learn how to overcome the lack of support. Throughout this book, we explain the underlying philosophies that make selling effective. Understanding these philosophies will help you defend and support your business development ideas with sound, logical reasons.

▼ Learn how to be an advocate for your selling effort.

If you still can't gain the support of your colleagues, you may have to come out of your own pocket for your business development effort. You may have to pay the membership dues to an organization, or for meals with prospects. However, in the long run, your ability to bring in business will help you earn more money and it will also help you overcome the lack of support. It is the golden rule of business:

"The person who brings in the gold makes the rules."

As a rainmaker, you will bring in more income. This will give you greater power to do what you want. And, if you are still unable to convince your colleagues, having the ability to generate business gives you the freedom to leave.

28. The force of inertia:

"I don't know where to begin."

If you haven't been doing much selling, then getting started can be difficult. The solution is to plan and implement small, achievable steps. Remember, selling is a process. As you take steps, acknowledge each intermediate success, even small ones. Ultimately, as you do more things, you will develop momentum and the process becomes easier to maintain.

Conclusion

Clearly, there are valid reasons for your reluctance to sell. You probably have experienced many of these. And, you may have encountered others that aren't mentioned here. But, don't allow your negative voice to stop you from selling. There are safe and effective methods that will keep you in your comfort zone. If you get into the habit of staying focused on selling, you can find the techniques that are both safe and effective for you.

Understand the Benefits of Selling | **3**

Some people will say that they don't need to sell
Life seems good without it, they're doing quite well.
But luck can change quickly, so we take the view
That learning to sell is the safe thing to do.

THE PURPOSE OF THIS CHAPTER is to spark your interest in selling. The more excited you are about selling, the more willing you will be to give it your consistent, constructive attention.

In Chapter 1, we gave you a formula called AAMAS (Attention leads to Awareness leads to Motivation leads to Action leads to Success). The formula begins with attention.

The Cost-Benefit Analysis of Selling

Your willingness to give selling your attention essentially comes down to a cost-benefit analysis in which the benefits of selling exceed your cost. Your cost includes time, money, inconvenience, and the risk of unpleasant feelings. When you perceive the benefits to be high, and your cost low, you will be more likely to give selling your attention.

The majority of this book is devoted to helping you reduce your *cost*, or discomfort with selling. We actually endeavor to help enjoy the selling process.

Our goal in *this* chapter is to help you understand the importance of selling. Once you understand its importance, you are more likely to make time for it and give it your consistent, constructive attention.

Upon fully appreciating the benefits of selling, we have seen people completely transform their attitudes and become passionate and vigorous in their selling efforts. As one of our clients stated: "I have come to see that selling is really 'Job one.' I don't know why I didn't see this before. But, now that I recognize this is the case, it's all I think about."

The Risk of Losing Clients Is Always Present

It is a common view that if you are busy today, you will always be busy. It is easy to have a false sense of security. But, things are always changing. Your contacts move. Your clients go out of business. Your clients may be bought out by companies that have relationships with other providers. Your competition may become more aggressive. Industries go through radical changes. Regardless of how busy or successful you are today, things can easily change.

▼

It is easy to get lulled into a false sense of security.

Learn from the Mistakes of Other Professionals

A client of ours, who works in a large law firm, was getting a steady stream of work from his partners. He assumed that the status quo would always remain and so he never did anything to build his practice. Then reality struck. A series of events took place that resulted in stopping the flow of new business. The economy changed and less business came to his firm. His colleagues, who began to feel the pinch, started keeping more of the work for themselves. And then, the firm hired younger, less expensive professionals to handle whatever work was available.

With our help, he dedicated his efforts to learn how to sell. We taught him how to put on seminars. We taught him how to reach out through networking. Now, he never forgets the importance of selling and he thinks about it all of the time. He has come to realize that no matter how busy he is with work, he must continue to focus on building for the future.

We had another client in the real estate law profession with over a $2 million book of business. As a result, he was earning a substantial income. He felt secure. But, his entire book of business was with only one client. One day, without warning, and just prior to coming to us, his client left him. Overnight, his entire book of business disappeared. It took over five years to build up his book to a respectable amount but nowhere near the $2 million book of business that he originally had.

Selling Can Be a Long-Term Process

Selling often requires a long time before you see success. It can take several years to develop new relationships. The timing must be right. It is a mistake to assume that you can simply go out and develop new business whenever you need it. No matter how busy and success-ful you are now, you must always be thinking about what could happen when things change. As one of our clients so wisely stated, "Your only financial security is your ability to gener-ate business."

▼

Ignoring your selling effort is dangerous and irresponsible.

The Benefits of Selling

It is not just the risk of loss that makes selling so important. There are tremendous benefits to be gained from selling. The more aware you are of the benefits, the more motivated you will be to focus on selling.

Money

The people who bring in business almost always make the most money. While in the past, companies may have compensated people based on their tenure, the trend has changed. People are more often compensated for the business they generate.

Power

Business developers also have the most power. One of our clients observed, "As long as I serve the clients of other partners in the firm, I am treated like a slave. The only way to have authority is to have my own book of business."

Freedom

Successful rainmakers generate business and delegate most of it to other people, retaining only the most interesting responsibilities for themselves. This gives them the freedom to do other things.

Job Security

Business generators are highly sought after. There are many fine techni-cians who can do the work. But, it is much easier to find good technicians than it is to find good business generators. This is not to say that doing good work isn't important. Nothing we talk about in this book is intended to minimize the value of doing good work. But, good work alone is not enough to guarantee success.

Self-Esteem

Another important benefit of selling is self-esteem. As your selling skills improve, so will your self-confidence. Also, the more success you experience, the better you will feel about yourself. The experience of closing deals is the equivalent of people saying: "I like you. I trust you."

Better Clientele

Another benefit of selling is higher quality clientele. No matter how successful you are, chances are that you have clients who are difficult, who don't pay their bills on time, who you don't like or respect, who are overly demanding and under-appreciative.

Difficult clients make it seem like a chore to come to work. They take the pleasure away from your job. They sap your energy. We call this the problem of the "golden handcuffs." You are stuck with your undesirable clients because you can't afford to let them go.

▼

Selling helps you get rid of the golden handcuffs.

Quality clients, on the other hand, give you energy. You look forward to interacting with them. They build your sense of pride and self-esteem. Selling gives you the ability to find more of the quality clients and say good-bye to your less desirable ones.

Momentum

Momentum is another benefit. The more selling you do, the easier it becomes. There is also a compounding effect that makes your selling more successful. As you do more things, people hear about you in different ways. It all adds up over time. The more well-known you are, the easier it is to get speaking and writing opportunities. The more people you know, the more exposure you have to their contacts. There is momentum.

Team Spirit

Another benefit of selling is team spirit. If you work in a firm, you may have partners who either know your contacts or other contacts at the companies you are targeting. In that case, you can work together to develop strategies for pursuing your prospects.

Working together for a common goal can be a bonding experience. It goes back to a time when our primitive hunter/gatherer ancestors worked together to feed and protect their tribes. It is a deeply engrained instinct that engenders camaraderie and team spirit.

One of our clients commented, "Working as a team to sell feels like a hunting party. We work together and plan together. It is fun and bonding, and then we get to share the rewards."

Doing Well by Doing Good

Many of our clients have discovered the benefits of doing well by doing good. Later in this book, we describe ways of getting involved in non-profit organizations as a way of generating business. These organizations can have an additional benefit of profound emotional fulfillment. There are so many worthy causes that allow you to help people in need. Our clients are involved in health-related organizations that help raise money for the cure of diseases. They are involved in organizations that raise money for the hungry. They raise money for medical relief in other countries. They join boards for local theatres, orchestras, and museums. They are involved in their children's schools. In fact, many of our clients have reported that their efforts in these types of organizations would have been worthwhile even without the benefits of generating new business.

We recommended that one client join a local food bank. He got on the board and said it was the one of the smartest things he has ever done in his life. He has made new friends. He has helped raise millions of dollars to feed the homeless. Eventually, he met some very influential people who became clients. But, he said, "Even if I hadn't gotten work, it would have been worth it."

▼
Doing good works can have profound emotional fulfillment.

Enjoyment

In time, as you experiment with different selling methods, you will probably find techniques that are not only comfortable, but that are enjoyable. One of our clients was initially extremely uncomfortable promoting his services. He had the classic misconception that selling involved doing things that were sleazy. Then we introduced him to public speaking. We invited him to speak at group of business people and he had a wonderful time. He became so excited about doing public speaking that it completely changed his life. Not only was it an effective business development technique, but it brought him great joy. Now, he seizes opportunities to speak whenever he gets the chance.

▼
The more enjoyable something is, the more you will give it your consistent, constructive attention.

For many people we know, bringing in new clients is an exhilarating experience. We have often had the pleasure of hearing our clients describe the experience of their bringing in their first new client. It's exciting and even addictive. Once bitten by the new business development bug, you will feel motivated to bring in more.

Intellectual Gratification

There is another significant benefit of selling that you may not have ever considered and that is that selling can be intellectually gratifying. There is a common myth that selling is for people who are not intellectually equipped to do anything better. But, it is just not true.

We have many clients who love selling who have graduated at the tops of their classes from some of the most prestigious schools. Developing quality relationships with people requires great mental discipline. It requires careful analysis of strategies and timing. Some of the techniques can become extremely sophisticated. It requires the ability to write and speak clearly. So, contrary to myth, selling is intellectually demanding and gratifying.

Keep Reviewing the Benefits

We recommend that you keep a list of all of the benefits that selling brings so that you can continually remind yourself of its importance. As you become more successful in selling, you will get busy, and there is risk of becoming complacent. Be aware of this temptation. You can never afford to let your selling efforts dwindle. The challenge is to learn how to sell when you are busy. This is the best time. When you are busy, you feel strong and confident.

> When you get busy, there is the risk of complacency.

Never forget that things can change suddenly. Clients leave, sometimes without warning. It takes time to build new relationships. Selling is always a priority.

Conclusion

This chapter described many of the benefits of selling. There may be more that you will discover. Hopefully, becoming aware of these benefits will spark and maintain your interest in selling.

Strategies That Keep You in Your Comfort Zone

Develop Confidence in Your Ability to Offer Value

4

If you balk when you sell
Don't assume you're not able.
You may not be proud of
What you bring to the table.
Selling becomes easy
When you honestly feel
The thing you are selling
Is a really good deal.

DEVELOPING GENUINE CONFIDENCE in your ability to offer value is one of the requirements for selling in your comfort zone. Confidence in the value you offer allows you to stay in your comfort zone by increasing your expectations of safety and effectiveness.

Safety

Confidence that you offer value increases your expectation of safety because it allows you to sell in ways that are honorable. There is no need to exaggerate or misrepresent your qualities. You don't have to be pushy or manipulative, or do anything that feels abusive. You don't have to change your personality. If you are an introvert, you don't have to become an extrovert.

Also, confidence that you offer value protects your self-esteem. When you genuinely believe that you offer something that people want and/or need, you are less likely to be afraid of rejection or embarrassment. Selling is so much more enjoyable when you know that you offer value.

Effectiveness

People who are confident in what they offer are more effective in motivating their prospects. There are several reasons for this. One reason is that confidence in the value you offer leads to greater enthusiasm about sharing that value with other people. Enthusiasm is contagious. The more enthusiastic you feel about what you offer, the more likely others will feel enthusiastic as well.

Enthusiasm also leads to greater persistent in your selling effort. And, persistence increases the likelihood of your success.

Finally, genuine confidence comes from having an in-depth understanding of how you offer value. The more you understand the value you offer, the easier it is to explain it to other people.

The relationship between confidence and your comfort zone is represented in Figure 2.

Figure 2

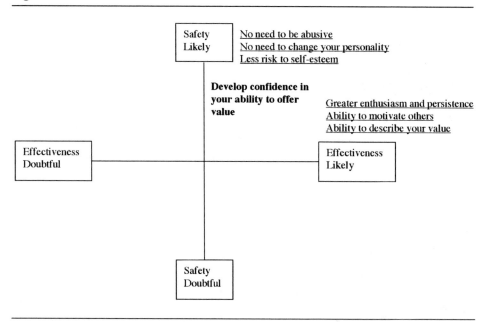

Confidence Requires Proof

It is well-accepted by many professionals that offering value is fundamental to successfully selling your services. But, what is *not* well-known is how to develop *confidence* in your ability to offer value. Simple self-affirmations such as "I offer value," are probably not enough to convince you. Genuine confidence in the value you offer requires proving to yourself that you offer a good deal. In this chapter, we give you techniques for evaluating and improving the quality of your deal.

The Obstacles to Developing Confidence

Professionals are often not in the habit of focusing on the value they offer. For example, when a client comes to you with a problem, you may handle it and then move on to the next problem, without reflecting on the value you just delivered. When you don't pay attention to the value you offer, you are less likely to notice it. As a result, you probably offer more value than you realize.

If you are modest, you may even minimize the value you offer. We had a client who was bright and highly skilled in his profession. He had graduated magna cum laude from Harvard University. His colleagues and clients raved about his work. But, he was unwilling to acknowledge his positive qualities. He said that as a child he had learned that self-praise was inappropriate. As a result, he found it difficult to think about the value he offered.

Not only did he ignore his own positive qualities, he believed that many of his competitors were highly skilled and offered quality service. This combination of minimizing his own value, and noticing that of his competitors made him feel inferior and uncomfortable with selling.

For purposes of selling in your comfort zone, it is imperative that you become aware of both the ways you currently offer value and how to improve your deal. This doesn't mean being conceited or self-centered. You don't need to brag or boast. At this point, we are purely interested in helping you develop a clear understanding of the value you offer. Later, you can decide which qualities, if any, you wish to reveal.

Three Factors Influencing Your Confidence

Your level of confidence in the value you offer comes from having an awareness of three factors:

1. The benefits you offer
2. The expectations of your clients
3. The benefits offered by your competition.

1. Reflect on the Benefits You Offer

The first step in developing confidence is to reflect on the benefits you offer. You can think of your confidence as a formula.

> $$C = B - F$$
>
> Confidence equals your awareness
> of benefits minus fees

The more benefits you are aware of offering in relationship to the fees you charge, the more confidence you will have that you offer a good deal. There are two categories of benefits: monetary and non-monetary.

Monetary benefits

One of the easiest ways to develop confidence in your ability to offer value is to identify your monetary benefits. Monetary benefits are easy to measure in the confidence formula described above.

For example, if you are a CPA who saves a client $20,000 in taxes and you charge $6,000 for your services, then you know that, at minimum, you offer $14,000 worth of value. Whenever possible, you should try to quantify value in terms of money.

> ✎ Comfort zone task—Make a list of the ways you help your clients earn or save money.

Non-monetary benefits

However, many types of benefits cannot be measured in terms of money. A psychologist may help someone improve self-esteem. A physician may help patients improve their health. An insurance agent may offer clients peace of mind. A lawyer may protect clients from getting sued. An architect may give clients the joy of living in a beautiful environment. While these benefits have great value, it is difficult to measure them in terms of money.

> ✎ Comfort zone task—Make a list of the non-monetary benefits you offer.

Examine Your Service

A useful technique for evaluating the non-monetary benefits you offer is to examine the elements of your service that create benefits. As we mentioned earlier, professionals are often not aware of the benefits of their services. Professionals tend to focus on doing a good job for their clients without reflecting on the specific benefits they offer. To be genuinely confident that you offer a good deal, you need to deconstruct the benefits of your service into two main components: your personal qualities and your systems.

Reflect on Your Personal Qualities

As a provider of professional services, your personal qualities are an intrinsic component of the value you offer. Reflect on your personal qualities which allow you to provide good service.

> Are you an expert or authority in your field?
> Are you attentive to the needs of your clients?
> Are you a good listener?
> Do you give sensible advice?
> Are you accessible?
> Are you responsive?
> Are you organized?
> Are you efficient?
> Are you trustworthy?
> Are you loyal?
> Are you empathic?
> Do you have good communication skills?

These are only a few examples of positive personal traits that you may possess. The table below lists important qualities. Which traits do *you* possess?

Positive Personal Traits

❑ Accessible	❑ Creative	❑ Honorable	❑ Punctual
❑ Accurate	❑ Decisive	❑ Humorous	❑ Reasonable
❑ Aggressive	❑ Discreet	❑ Imaginative	❑ Reliable
❑ Attentive	❑ Efficient	❑ Inquisitive	❑ Respectful
❑ Calm	❑ Empathic	❑ Insightful	❑ Responsible
❑ Careful	❑ Enthusiastic	❑ Inspirational	❑ Responsive
❑ Caring	❑ Experienced	❑ Intelligent	❑ Sensible
❑ Cautious	❑ Flexible	❑ Knowledgeable	❑ Sincere
❑ Compassionate	❑ Friendly	❑ Loyal	❑ Solution-Oriented
❑ Confident	❑ Generous	❑ Observant	❑ Tactful
❑ Conscientious	❑ Genuine	❑ Organized	❑ Talented
❑ Cooperative	❑ Hard-working	❑ Patient	❑ Thoughtful
❑ Cost-Conscious	❑ Helpful	❑ Persistent	❑ Trustworthy
❑ Courteous	❑ Honest	❑ Positive	❑ Wise

Think about your other positive personal qualities. The more aware you become of your positive personal qualities, the more confidence you will have in the value you offer, and the more comfortable you will become with selling.

Develop Your Personal Qualities

After reflecting on your personal qualities, you may decide that certain traits need improvement. Here are some tips for improving personal qualities.

> ✎ Comfort zone task—Make a list of your positive personal qualities. Keep adding to it. Build your confidence in your personal qualities.

Knowledge and expertise

As a provider of professional services, two essential qualities are knowledge and expertise. The more knowledgeable and skilled you believe you are, the more confidence you will have in your ability to offer value. Here are some techniques for improving knowledge and expertise.

Participate in the trade groups of your clients

Get involved in your clients' trade organizations. Go to their educational programs. Read their publications. You may even want to take a leadership role on their committees. The more interest you take in their trade organizations, the more knowledgeable you will become in the issues that impact their businesses.

Write articles

It sounds counter-intuitive to write about something that you are trying to learn. After all, you need to know about it to write about it. However, once you have a basic understanding about an issue, writing an article helps you understand the nuances. It forces you to think through issues and understand them more thoroughly. It also helps you explain issues more clearly and concisely. Many people agree that you don't really know a topic until you have written about it.

> ✎ Comfort zone task—Write an article on a topic with which you have some familiarity.

Of course, there are obstacles to writing articles. You have to think of a good topic and you have to allocate the time and effort. But, we believe that it is well worth the investment. We provide many tips for overcoming the obstacles to writing articles in Skill Module C: Tips for effective and affordable public relations.

Do public speaking

Public speaking is another technique for increasing your knowledge. There is an old saying that if you want to learn about something, teach it. Preparing a topic for a group of clients or other professionals in your area of expertise will force you to become an authority. We provide tips for public speaking in Skill Module 1: Tips for Public Speaking.

Collaborate

We encourage you to collaborate on articles and speeches with people who you respect. Collaborating with other people creates an opportunity to exchange and challenge each other's ideas. As a result, you both come away with much greater insight and understanding of the issues.

Develop other personal traits

In addition to your knowledge and expertise, you can improve other personal traits such as creativity, imagination, flexibility, and patience. We have clients who have taken courses in acting, comedy, music, and creative writing. The traits they nurtured as a result of these activities were highly useful in providing value to their clients.

Evaluate Your Systems

Another method of building confidence in the value of your service is to review your systems for insuring quality service. Your systems can include the following components:

- Guiding principles (or philosophies of doing business)
- Policies and procedures
- Staff
- Training
- Technology

Guiding principles

Your guiding principles, or philosophies for doing business, are the underlying beliefs that guide your decisions about how you help your clients. A litigator whose guiding principle is to help clients keep their costs down will always advise the most cost-effective course of action. Instead of immediately litigating, he might first recommend negotiation or mediation.

When we coach people in sales, our guiding principle is that you should always strive to stay in your comfort zone. We believe that this is the most effective way to help you get results. Everything we advise is based on this philosophy. We teach you how to build confidence in your ability to offer value. We help you identify targets you will feel comfortable reaching out to. We show you comfortable ways of communicating with your targets. Every step that we teach is based on the guiding principle of staying in your comfort zone.

Take a moment now and reflect on *your* guiding principles. When you believe that your guiding principles are sound, this will help to increase your confidence that you offer value.

✎ Comfort zone task—Identify and evaluate the philosophies that guide your practice.

Policies and procedures

Your policies and procedures are the rules that insure quality service. Knowing that you have good policies and procedures will increase your confidence in your ability to offer value.

For example, many of our clients have adopted the "24-hour call back policy." This means that if they are not available when someone calls, either they, or someone from their office will call back within 24 hours. This policy insures responsiveness and accessibility.

We have a client who is proud of her accuracy and efficiency. Her procedure is that prior to submitting documents to her clients, every document is reviewed with a checklist to make sure that everything necessary is included. This procedure gives her great confidence in the value that she offers.

In our company, we are proud of our punctuality. To ensure this quality, we use the most accurate clocks available. These clocks are reset by a daily radio transmission from the atomic clock in Colorado. When we have an appointment to call someone, we follow the procedure of dialing a few seconds prior to the appointment. People who know us are consistently impressed with our punctuality and we have become well-known for this quality.

> ✒ Comfort zone task—Make a list of your policies and procedures for insuring quality service.

Staff

Another way to build confidence in your service is to hire staff that makes you proud. Always strive to hire people with good character who share your values. And, have the courage to let people go who are either unable or refuse to adopt your core philosophies. Many of our clients were unable to sell until they hired and took pride in their staff.

> ✒ Comfort zone task—Identify the characteristics of your staff members that make you feel proud.

Training

To ensure quality service, you should make training a priority. When your employees are well-trained, you will feel more confident in their ability and enthusiastic about promoting your service.

Obviously, you want them to be skilled in doing their work. But also, you want them to mirror your principles and philosophies. We recommend holding regular "best practices" meetings in which you discuss not only methods of doing their work, but your underlying beliefs. In this way, your employees are more likely to mirror your principles and philosophies to your clients.

For example, if being flexible is an underlying philosophy for providing good service, then you should discuss the elements of being flexible. What does it mean to be flexible? Why is it important to clients? And how do you communicate flexibility to clients so that they appreciate that you possess this quality?

> ▼
> ✎ Comfort zone task—Identify the skills, principles and philosophies you want your staff to learn.

Technology

Many professionals find it difficult to embrace new technology. New technology can be frightening and difficult to learn. And sometimes, new technology doesn't work as promised. So, it may feel more comfortable to cling to old ways.

However, refusing to consider new technology can minimize your ability to offer quality service. And, if your competitors are improving their technology, this could put you at a severe disadvantage.

> ▼
> ✎ Comfort zone task—Stay alert to technology that can improve your service.

Make sure that you are aware of technology that allows you to provide the highest quality service. The more confident you are that you are using high-quality technology; the more comfortable you will feel with selling your services.

Capture Your Observations

If you are not in the habit of thinking about the quality of your service, then developing this awareness may take some time and practice. To help you improve your ability to focus on value, we have created the tool called the "Capture Your Observations" form shown in Exhibit A. Make copies of the form and keep them in a place where you can easily find them. Throughout the day, try to notice the things you do that offer value to your clients, and write them down.

If you are consistent in capturing your observations, you will accumulate a collection of examples of techniques that prove your ability to offer value. This habit will also increase your selling awareness. You will start noticing new ideas for providing value. You will notice how other people offer value.

> ▼
> ✎ Comfort zone task—Print out the "Capture Your Observations" form and document the benefits you offer.

For example, we know a consultant who adopted a new pricing technique that he learned from his piano instructor. The instructor provided volume discounts by lowering his rate after a certain number of hours were purchased. Upon observing this technique,

Exhibit A—Capture Your Observations Form

OBSERVATION: _____ DATE:_____

NOTES:_____

_____

_____

OBSERVATION: _____ DATE:_____

NOTES:_____

_____

_____

OBSERVATION: _____ DATE:_____

NOTES:_____

_____

_____

OBSERVATION: _____ DATE:_____

NOTES:_____

_____

_____

OBSERVATION: _____ DATE:_____

NOTES:_____

_____

_____

OBSERVATION: _____ DATE:_____

NOTES:_____

_____

_____

OBSERVATION: _____ DATE:_____

NOTES:_____

_____

_____

OBSERVATION: _____ DATE:_____

NOTES:_____

_____

_____

our client wrote it down, and he later used tiered discounts successfully with his own clients.

It will only take you a moment to write down the thought and capture it for life. But, if you don't, it is likely that you will forget it. A thought not written down may be lost forever.

Ask Yourself, "Is There a Better Way?"

One way to improve the quality of your service is to get into the habit of asking yourself, "Is there a better way?" In our business, we developed our current model for helping people by consistently asking ourselves this question.

When we started helping people market their services, we began with traditional approaches that were commonly used at the time. These traditional approaches included methods such as conducting seminars and doing strategic planning. But, over the years, we kept asking ourselves whether or not we believed that the traditional approaches were really the best. Consistently, we challenged our methodologies and philosophies. We experimented with new techniques and models. Gradually, we developed our current model, which provides additional support. Now, in addition to seminars and strategic planning, we coach our clients over the telephone in individual, confidential meetings.

After testing this methodology, we have proved that our approach is the most likely to help people change their behavior and achieve their goals. While we still believe there is a place for the traditional approaches, we are absolutely certain that our innovative approach gives our clients the greatest benefit for the money. And, this confidence gives us the motivation to enthusiastically and successfully promote our way of doing business.

Even so, we still try to find ways to improve our service because we know that the competition is always getting smarter, and our clients are becoming more sophisticated. Developing and maintaining confidence in the value that you offer requires that you consistently strive to improve your service.

2. Identify Your Clients' Expectations

In addition to your own observations about the value you offer, your confidence is dependent upon what your clients expect from you. To sell in your comfort zone, it is imperative that you find out what their expectations are. Once you genuinely are convinced that you are meeting your clients' expectations, this will dramatically increase your confidence in your deal.

Ask for Client Feedback

The best way to identify your client expectations is to ask them for feedback. Select a few clients whose opinions you trust and ask them about the quality of service you are providing. Often, people who think that they are doing a good job for their clients are surprised to learn that they are falling short in a variety of areas.

For example, one of our clients was certain that he was doing the best possible job for his clients. He hired us to do a survey for several of his best clients. Every client surveyed said that they were unsatisfied with his familiarity of their particular industries. Upon receiving this feedback, he immediately corrected the problem. He joined his clients' trade associations, attended their meetings, and subscribed to their magazines. His efforts to improve this area of his service not only fixed the problem, but dramatically sparked his enthusiasm to reach out to new people in those industries.

How to ask for feedback from clients

You can ask your clients for feedback in several ways. The easiest and most direct method is simply to ask them immediately after doing some work for them. You might say, "I just want to take a moment and confirm that you are satisfied with the quality of our service." It has been our experience that clients are usually happy to take a moment and tell you about their level of satisfaction.

> ▼
> ✎ Comfort zone task—Ask clients for feedback immediately after completing some work.

Implement client satisfaction surveys

If you feel awkward about directly asking your clients for feedback, then you can do client satisfaction surveys. Surveys can be conducted by a third party and can obtain extensive feedback that will help you improve your service.

For more information on obtaining client feedback, refer to *Skill Module 5: Tips for client satisfaction surveys*.

Implement lost opportunity interviews

You can learn about your prospective clients' expectations by doing "lost opportunity interviews." When a potential client declines your proposal or even when you lose a client, you should find out the reasons why. Ask your clients and prospects why they went with someone else. This may help you learn about areas in which you could do a better job offering value in the future.

Give Added-Benefits

When your clients hire you, they have certain expectations about the quality and cost of your work. Clearly, you want to meet their expectations. But, we believe that whenever possible, you should exceed client expectations.

Don't get stuck in the habit of simply doing the work. Good work is important, but it is only one component of the value you offer. Remember the confidence formula described earlier. Benefits minus fees equals confidence in your ability to offer value. The more benefits you are aware of offering in relationship to the fees you charge, the more confidence you will have in the value you offer. Ideally, you want the benefits to far outweigh the fees. In other words, you should be confident that you offer a really great deal.

> ▼
> A great deal is when the benefits you offer far outweigh the fees you charge.

The Five Categories of Added-Benefits

What added-benefits can you give your clients? Depending on the nature of your work and relationships with your clients, there may be many types of added-benefits that you can provide. Here are five main categories:

- Education
- Entertainment
- Introductions
- Leadership
- Inspiration

Education

Clients expect a certain amount of education as a part of the work you do for them. They expect you to help them understand the problems they are facing, and they want your advice. But, there are many more ways that you can educate your clients. For example, many professionals give the added-benefit of conducting seminars for their clients. Or they write articles and newsletters, and then disseminate these publications to their clients. The more you help your clients by giving them interesting and useful information, the more confidence you will have in your ability to offer value.

> ▼
> ✎ Comfort zone task—Make a list of some topics for seminars and articles that would benefit your clients.

Entertainment

Entertainment is a common added-benefit. People like to have fun. Often, clients highly value meals, ballgames, the theater, and parties.

We had a client who enjoys auto racing and invites his clients to go to the race track. We have had many clients who love classical music and regularly bring their clients to concerts. Think of things that *you* like to do and consider inviting your clients to participate. Entertainment gives value to your clients, and helps strengthen your relationships.

> ✒ Comfort zone task—Think of activities you enjoy that would be appreciated by clients.

Introductions

> ✒ Comfort zone task—Identify the people you know who would benefit your clients.

Many professionals regularly give the added-benefit of making introductions. Perhaps you know a good lawyer, accountant, or banker who could be of value to your clients. You may have colleagues within your own organization who can provide other services that could benefit your contacts.

Join a networking group to expand your ability to make introductions. Networking groups can provide access to other professionals with a wide range of expertise who you can introduce to your clients.

> ✒ Comfort zone task—Locate organizations that can help you build your network of quality professionals.

Leadership

Another type added-benefit is leadership. You may be able to take a leadership role in the lives of your clients. For example, maybe you can get active in their trade and professional organizations. By going to their meetings and joining committees, you are taking an active interest in their businesses and learning more about the issues that impact their lives. You

> ✒ Comfort zone task—Identify the organizations that your clients support.

can also get involved in the non-profit charities and community organizations that you clients care about. Not only will this give added-benefit to your clients, but it can be personally fulfilling, give you the ability to spend time with your clients, and help you meet new people.

Inspiration

This is one of the hidden benefits that you may offer. Many professionals do not think of themselves as being inspirational. But, the fact is, everyone we know either is or can be more inspirational. This is because we define inspiration as the ability to instill self-confidence. Whenever you act as a sounding board and let clients tell you about obstacles they are facing, that's inspirational. When you give your clients advice that reveals a pathway for overcoming the obstacles they are facing, that's inspirational.

> ▼
> 🖎 Comfort zone task—Be aware of opportunities to be inspirational.

3. Identify Your Competition's Benefits

A third factor in developing confidence that you offer value is to compare your deal to the competition. Developing confidence in the value you offer requires proving to yourself that you offer a superior deal.

Do some reconnaissance to find out about what your competition offers. Information about your competitors is not always readily available. However, there are some ways of obtaining it. One method is to ask people you trust who have had interaction with your competitors. Perhaps you have clients and friends who have done business with your competitors.

You may be able to go to programs where you competitors are speaking. Or check out their promotional materials on their Web sites.

Make a Comparison

Once you acquire information about your competition, the next step is to make a comparison. The obvious way to compare your services is by how much you charge. But, remember, value is comprised of many qualities of which money is only a part. So, avoid falling into this trap. We have many clients who are the highest priced providers in their markets, but who are still confident that they offer the best deal.

Even if you charge more than the competition you still may provide benefits that make you the preferred provider. Think about the meaningful

> ▼
> You may charge more than the competition and still offer a superior deal.

things that differentiate you from your competitors. Consider all of the things we have discussed in this chapter, including your positive personal traits, your systems for ensuring quality service, and all of the benefits that you offer.

Become Proud of the Fees You Charge

Ideally, you should develop your confidence to a level that you are proud to quote your fees. This may seem odd to you at first. After all, who is enthusiastic talking about fees? We know professionals who are actually embarrassed to quote their fees. They suspect that they might be overcharging their clients, or that the competition offers a better deal. However, once you become genuinely confident that you offer a superior deal to the competition, you will be proud of the fees you charge.

Conclusion

The purpose of this chapter has been to help you gain genuine confidence that you offer a good deal. The more confident you are that the benefits you offer outweigh the fees you charge, the more comfortable with selling you will become. You will feel secure in the knowledge that you can sell honorably, without bragging, boasting, or using abusive techniques. And, equally important, you will be more successful because confidence that you offer value leads to greater enthusiasm, persistence, and ability to communicate the value that you offer.

Identify Targets in Your Comfort Zone

5

As you watch all your contacts accruing
The value of each needs reviewing.
With your limited time,
It would be such a crime
To invest in those not worth pursuing.

THE NEXT STRATEGY for selling in your comfort zone is to identify targets in your comfort zone. In the previous chapter, we discussed strategies for developing confidence in your ability to offer value. Now, we turn our attention to the process of identifying the targets with whom you plan to communicate.

Some people may be concerned that word "target" is aggressive or predatory. However, we are using it merely as a generic term to describe a wide-range of individuals who might be influenced or changed by your actions. Targets may include clients, prospects, referral sources, program chairs, publishers, editors, and other people that can help you in your business development effort. By using the word target, we avoid having to repeat all of these sub-categories.

If you can locate highly qualified targets, then you will be well on your way to success. Of course, you still need to decide how to communicate the value that you offer. But, it is much easier to sell to people once you know that they are the right people.

To stay in your comfort zone, we recommend that you always strive to find targets that meet the following two comfort criteria:

1. They should have the potential to lead to new business.
2. You should like them.

As illustrated in Figure 3, focusing on meeting targets that satisfy these two criteria will increase your comfort with selling. When you are confident that your targets are likely to lead to new business, you will feel more justified in investing your time and money. And, when you like your targets, the experience will be more enjoyable.

Figure 3

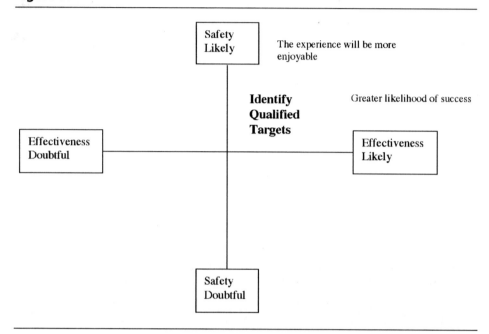

Comfort Criterion #1: Identify Targets with the Potential to Lead to New Business

Pursuing targets that have a high potential to lead to new business will increase your confidence that you are investing your time and money wisely.

There are three categories of targets with this potential: prospects, referral sources, and resources.

Prospects

Prospects are your potential clients. Quality prospects have the following three characteristics:

1. They have a need for your services.
2. They can afford your services.
3. They have the decision-making authority to retain your services.

Referral Sources

Referral sources are people who can introduce you to your prospects. Quality referral sources have the following *two* characteristics:

1. They know your ideal prospects.
2. They have credibility in the minds of their contacts.

Resources

Resources are people who can advise you and/or assist you in meeting your ideal prospects and referral sources. It might be someone who is knowledgeable in selling who could give you suggestions for how to meet and build business relationships with prospects and referral sources. Or, it might be someone who could assist you in getting speaking, article writing, and networking opportunities in organizations that provide you with entrée to prospects and referral sources.

Comfort Criterion #2: Identify Targets That You Like

Whenever possible, we believe that you should try to identify targets that you like. This may seem like a touchy/feely sentiment to find in a business book. Nevertheless, we believe that it is an important targeting criterion. This book is all about selling in your comfort zone. The more you like your targets, the more likely you are to enjoy selling to them. And, as we pointed out in Chapter 1, the more you enjoy selling, the more willing you will be to give it your consistent, constructive attention. The more attention you provide, the more likely you are to succeed.

We had a client who said that he hated the idea of socializing with his clients. He didn't share their interests, and he found them to be rude and sarcastic. And yet, he felt that it was necessary to socialize with them to keep their business. The thought of generating more of the same types of clients was unappealing. So, he didn't make the effort. We were able to help him target a different caliber of clientele—one that he liked and enjoyed spending time with. This shift in his targeting completely transformed his attitude, and he began to embrace selling enthusiastically.

Identify Qualities about Your Targets That You Like

We realize that identifying targets that you like is not always possible. But, it is a standard that you should always strive to achieve.

Look for people you feel that you can respect and trust, and who appreciate the value that you offer. This will lead to a greater feeling of safety as you spend time with them.

Keep in mind that you may know people with whom you currently don't feel comfortable because you don't know much about them. However, as you learn more about your contacts, you may find that you feel more connected to them.

One of the ways you can feel more connected to your targets is to learn about your targets' values and beliefs. You will feel more comfortable with people when you share fundamental beliefs.

Another way to feel more connected is to find out about their interests. We had a client who didn't like one of his prospects until he learned that they shared a mutual interest in bicycling. Upon making this discovery, he invited his prospect to join his bicycling group for a Sunday ride. They became friendly and later our client was hired.

Two Fundamental Strategies for Finding Your Targets

Finding qualified targets may be one of your biggest challenges. The world is a large place. It can be difficult to zero-in on the people who have the precise qualifications that you are looking for. Furthermore, your targets' needs, circumstances, and perceptions are continually changing.

There are two fundamental approaches to finding your best targets. One approach is to focus on people you have already met. The second approach is to focus on meeting strangers.

In this chapter, we help you build a target list of the people you have already met. In Chapter 8, we will give you some comfortable techniques for meeting strangers.

Begin with the People You Have Already Met

We always recommend that you begin your targeting effort by reviewing the names of your existing contacts. As we said earlier in this book, selling is a relationship-building process. It can take a long time to meet, get to know, and to build trust with people. The relationship-building process has already begun with the people you have met. By targeting existing contacts, your selling effort will be a more efficient and enjoyable experience.

▼
✎ Comfort zone task—Review the names of your existing contacts.

What If You Don't Know Many People?

If you don't know many people, then obviously you will have to meet new people. However, before jumping to the conclusion that you don't know many quality targets, make sure that you have made a thorough review of your existing contacts. You probably know more people than you can recall off the top of your head. If you haven't been doing much selling, then you probably don't have a comprehensive mailing list or contact database. Consequently, you probably will have forgotten many of the people you have met.

We had a client, in the beginning of our consulting relationship, who was adamant that he didn't know anyone worth pursuing for new business. Nevertheless, we urged him to look through his rolodex starting with the letter A. He wasn't comfortable with anyone under letter "A," so he moved to letter "B." Then, he suddenly exclaimed, "Oh yeah, I remember this person! I had forgotten about him. He is a great potential referral source. In fact, he had suggested that we have lunch about six months ago and I forgot to schedule it." He called the contact, they had lunch, and he got a substantial piece of business referred to him almost immediately after that lunch.

Often, target opportunities are all around you. Think of all the people you have had contact with over the course of your life, but with whom you haven't stayed in touch. You may have contacts from school or people you have met through work, and who might be able to assist you. But, because you weren't thinking about sales at the time you met them, you didn't consider these individuals as potential targets. Now, you can reconsider these relationships.

▼
Target opportunities may be all around you.

If you were to do a thorough review, you may be surprised at how many targets you actually know. It is possible that some of these contacts have grown stale because so much time has elapsed since you last communicated with them. One of the lessons that we teach in selling is the importance of staying in touch with contacts in order keep the doors of communication open. As you will see in Chapter 9, it doesn't really take very much to maintain a meaningful presence your contacts' lives. A holiday card once a year, a correspondence, or an occasional phone call may be enough to keep you top-of-mind.

But, if the doors are closed because you haven't stayed in touch, there still may be ways of opening them. We have been very successful in helping our clients find strategies for re-opening doors with relationships that have grown stale. You will find many of these communication strategies in Chapters 6 and 7. But, for now, your task is simply to identify all of the people you have met. We will focus on how to communicate with them and strengthen your business relationships later in this book.

Consider the following groups of people you have met who may have the potential of becoming prospects:

- Existing clients
- Past clients
- Colleagues
- Competitors
- Advisors
- Friends and family

Existing clients

Some of your best targets are existing clients. They are the easiest and most comfortable to communicate with because they have already experienced the value that you offer. If they have continuing needs for your services, they may be prospects for additional work. Satisfied clients can also be good referral sources. They may be able to introduce you to their friends and colleagues.

Past clients

You may have past clients who have additional needs for your services. As with existing clients, past clients have demonstrated a need for your services, and are therefore potential prospects. But, if they haven't heard from you in a while, they may not be thinking about you.

> ▼
> Past and current clients may have additional needs for your services.

Colleagues

If you work in a company or firm, you may have partners who would benefit from your ability to bring in business. They may have contacts and other resources that could help you become more successful. We have a client who is an estate-planning attorney in a small law firm who gets most of his business from CPAs. Our client's principal sales effort is encouraging his partners who practice other types of law to introduce him to their CPA contacts. This has been a highly effective strategy.

> ▼
> Your colleagues may have contacts you would like to meet.

Competitors

In some businesses, even competitors can be quality targets. Professionals frequently refer work to their competitors. Your competitors may run across situations which they can't handle for a variety of reasons. They may not have your specialized skills. The size of the request may be too small or too large. There may be conflicts of interest that prevent them from taking on a specific client. Or, they may be too busy to take on new clients.

> ▼
> Even your competitors may be good referral sources.

Advisors

Your advisors, such as your banker, accountant, lawyer, financial planner, and insurance agent, all come into contact with people who you may want to meet. You should also meet your clients' advisors. If you get work from a particular group, let's say CPAs, ask yourself, "Have you met all of the CPAs of all of your clients?"

> ▼
> Have you met all of the CPAs of all of your clients?

Friends and family

Your friends and family may be able to help you generate new business. Many of our clients do business with their friends and family. It can be both profitable and enjoyable.

What If You Are Uncomfortable Selling to Friends?

If you are like a lot of people, you may initially be uncomfortable with the idea of targeting your friends. And, in some cases you may be wise to avoid selling to friends. We have had many clients who have told us that they simply don't want to risk valued friendships by bringing up the subject of business. There is the risk of imposing on friends. There is the risk of revealing neediness. There is the risk that a business deal could damage friendships, especially if things don't work out well.

On the other hand, it would be unfortunate to eliminate the possibility of doing business with someone simply because he or she is a friend. Many of our clients say that their best clients are their friends.

The solution is to review the names of each of your friends to determine if your discomfort is justified. If you decide to do business with friends, there are many safe and effective ways of communicating with them. In Chapters 6 and 7, we provide these techniques.

> ▼
> Don't arbitrarily dismiss the possibility of doing business with friends.

With Practice, Your Comfort Zone Will Expand

As we mentioned earlier, your comfort zone is dynamic! As you gain practice in reaching out to people who you know and develop confidence in your communication skills, your comfort zone will expand. As this happens, you will feel more comfortable reaching out to people who initially you might not have felt comfortable contacting. So, it is important that you get into the habit of reviewing your contacts from time to time.

> ▼
> With time and practice, the number of contacts you feel comfortable reaching out to will expand.

Create a Target List

To initiate your targeting effort, we recommend that you document the names of all of people you have met who you believe may be quality targets. Go through your rolodex cards, business card files, address books, and any other places where you may keep the names of people who you have met. More specifically, look for the names of people who satisfy the two comfort criteria: You like them and believe that they are a potential prospect, referral source, and/or resource.

If you have a large number of existing contacts, this task may take some time. But, it is well worth your effort. Stick with it. Set time aside in your calendar for the task of adding names to your target list. There are many benefits of creating a target list.

1) Creating a target list is motivational.
2) A target list ensures that you remember names.
3) A target list helps you develop target awareness.

Creating a Target List Is Motivational

Since inertia is one of the common obstacles that you may be facing, creating a target list is usually one of the first steps that we recommend to our clients. After conducting thousands of coaching sessions with our clients, we have learned that creating a target list is highly motivational. Upon seeing the names of people who are within your comfort zone, there is a very good chance that you will feel motivated to contact them.

A Target List Ensures That You Remember Names

Another great benefit of maintaining a target list is that it prevents you from forgetting your targets. You may not necessarily be able to think of strategies right now to communicate with every target on your list, but at least you won't forget about them. Later, you can review your target list and in time, develop communication strategies.

It seems so basic for us to tell you to write names down. And yet, people don't write things down. At the time that you have someone's name in mind, it may be difficult to imagine that you won't remember that person later. But, the fact is, when you get busy, it is easy to forget even the most urgent things if they are not written down.

Several years ago, we were helping a high-profile lawyer with his marketing effort. During one of our consulting sessions, we helped him identify six of his best targets. But he was convinced that it wasn't necessary to write down their names. He said that he knew who his targets were and that he wouldn't forget them. So *we* wrote down the names. Two months later, we asked him again to give us the names of his six best targets. He gave us six different names. And we said, "What about these six?" And we read the list of names we had written down two months earlier. And he said, "I am embarrassed to admit it, but I forgot about them." From then on, he started documenting the names of his best targets.

A Target List Develops Target Awareness

One of the most significant benefits of documenting the names of your quality targets is that it helps you to develop target awareness. Creating a target list forces you to think about your best targets. As you get into the habit of thinking about your best targets, you will begin to notice potential targets that previously you may have ignored.

Think of the times when you've run into people you know at the store or the gym. Some of these acquaintances may have been potential targets for selling. But, because you weren't thinking about selling at the time, you probably didn't make that connection. Once you develop the habit of documenting your best targets, you develop a new sense of awareness. Every time you run into an acquaintance, ask yourself, "Is there a potential selling opportunity here?"

> ▼
> ✍ Comfort zone task—Create a target list of people you know.

Don't Put This Off

This seemingly simple task may actually prove to be one of the most important lessons of this book. So, don't put this off. You should start building your target list right now. This is a highly effective technique for overcoming your inertia, remembering important contacts, and developing target awareness.

Two Types of Target Lists

There are two distinct types of target lists that you should maintain:

1) A primary target list, and
2) A mailing list, or contact database

Your Primary Target List

Your primary target list includes the people you should contact first. These are the people who you like and who you believe have the highest potential of leading to new business.

Your Mailing List or Contact Database

Your mailing list or contact database includes all of your contacts, including your longer term targets. Selling is a numbers game. The more quality targets that you stay in touch with over time; the more likely you are to be successful in your selling effort. So, it makes sense to keep the names of all of your potential targets in your mailing list. Later, as you become more knowledgeable with the selling process, you can review your mailing list to determine whether or not to purge some of them.

Resist the Temptation to Omit Names from Your Contact Database

As you build your contact database, you will probably feel tempted to omit some of the names that you come across. You may not see them as worthwhile targets. Or, you may feel skeptical about your ability to approach them in a comfortable manner.

However, we urge you to resist the temptation dismiss names too quickly. Even if someone isn't a target right now, circumstances change. Over time, you may develop new services to offer. Your prospects' needs, authority, and financial situations may change. Their perceptions about the value that you offer may change.

Even prospects that are currently being served by your competition may be long-term targets and worth keeping in your mailing list. Your competitors may make mistakes. They could go out of business. You may have specialized skills that your competitors don't possess. Of course, if your prospects are happy with the competition, you shouldn't expect them to commit treason. But, should circumstances change, you want to be positioned in the minds of your targets as the next provider of choice.

> ▼
> You want to maintain a presence in the lives of your targets so that when the timing is right you are top-of-mind.

Having the names of your targets in a mailing list gives you the ability to stay in touch with your targets over a long period of time. This increases the likelihood that your targets will be thinking of you when the timing is right.

Conclusion

Identifying quality targets is a key to your staying in your comfort zone. You will feel more enthusiastic about reaching out to contacts when you feel that it is a worthwhile use of your time, and when you feel connected to them.

Begin by documenting the names of existing contacts. Later, in Chapter 8, we will show you comfortable methods for building your base of contacts.

Communicate Value to Your Targets

6

Although you feel proud of the things you sell,
If their value is secret, they won't sell well.
So your job is explaining the reasons to buy,
When folks understand them, they'll give them a try.

IN THE TWO PRECEDING CHAPTERS, we focused on two essential comfort zone strategies: developing confidence in your ability to offer value, and identifying quality targets. Now, we turn our attention to what we believe is the core of selling in your comfort zone: communicating value to quality targets. To sell in your comfort zone, you must develop communication strategies that give you a high expectation of safety and effectiveness.

Increase Your Expectation of Safety

In this chapter, we help you identify communication strategies that will increase your expectation of safety. Selling doesn't require the stereotypical behavior described in Chapter 2. You don't have to be pushy, sleazy, or abusive in any way. You don't have to feel awkward about selling. Rather, you have to learn how to communicate your ability to offer value. Communicating value gives you valid reasons for reaching out to your targets. It allows you to you feel good about yourself and proud of what you offer.

Increase Your Expectation of Effectiveness

You can increase your expectation of effectiveness by communicating the benefits you offer. By communicating benefits, you communicate two qualities that are particularly important for increasing your effectiveness: capability and compatibility.

Communicating capability is the process of inspiring confidence in your ability to help your targets. Communicating compatibility is the process of revealing your ability to work and communicate well with your targets. The more effective you are in communicating capability and compatibility, the more effective you will be in motivating your targets to hire you and refer you to their contacts.

The relationship between your comfort zone and comfortable communication strategies is reflected in Figure 4.

Figure 4

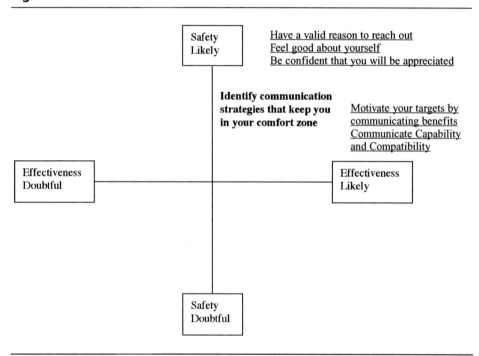

Review the Benefits You Offer

Before you can accurately communicate your ability to offer value, you must be clear about what that value is. Take a moment and review Chapter 4 and any notes you took which identify the benefits you offer.

Select the Benefits You Want to Communicate

Once you are clear about the benefits you offer, the next step is to decide which benefits you want to reveal. Keep in mind that whenever you communicate with someone, you reveal *something* about yourself. What you reveal may be positive or negative. It may be accurate or inaccurate. It may have been communicated intentionally or unintentionally. But, every communication reveals something. So, you may as well try to communicate the things you *want* people to know.

Think about the personal qualities you possess which you want your targets to notice. For example, you may want your targets to know that you are knowledgeable and skilled in your practice. Think about your systems—your guiding principles and procedures that insure quality service. From now on, every communication with your targets should have the goal of communicating these benefits, whether it is by phone, in-person, via the Internet, through your promotional materials, or through the media.

Three Mediums of Communication

There are three mediums for communicating the benefits you offer:

1. Your deeds
2. Your dialogue
3. Your documents

1. Your Deeds

The first medium for communicating value is your deeds or actions. It is often true that actions speak louder than words. Instead of merely talking about the value you offer, your actions allow people to experience it first hand. When people experience the value that you offer, they are more likely to understand and appreciate it.

Give "Value-in-Advance"

One of the most effective strategies for communicating value to your contacts is a strategy called "value-in-advance." Ever since we began consulting our clients in 1985, "value-in-advance" has proven to be the most significant concept for professionals to promote their services both safely and effectively.

> "Value-in-Advance" is one of the most important strategies for selling in your comfort zone.

"Value-in-advance" is the strategy of offering something for free as a way of allowing your targets to experience a sample of the benefits that you offer. If you were selling a product, then "value-in-advance" might be a sample of the product.

When Gillette Mach III came out, they sent out free razors and blades. Grocery stores regularly give away sample foods they want you to try. Giving free samples is a common retail marketing strategy. As a professional service provider, you should provide something of value that allows you to interact with your targets and paint a picture of what it is like to work with you.

▼

"Value-in-Advance" paints a picture of what it is like to work with you.

We divide "Value-in-Advance" into five main categories:

- Education
- Entertainment
- Introductions
- Leadership
- Inspiration

You may recognize these categories from our discussion on added-benefits in Chapter 4. The difference here is that instead of giving additional benefits to current clients, your goal is to give value to prospects and other targets as a way of demonstrating to them what it is like to work with you.

Giving "value-in-advance" helps you sell in your comfort zone because it increases your expectations of safety and effectiveness.

Safety

A fundamental reason why professionals are uncomfortable with selling is that asking for business feels embarrassing. It can feel needy, pushy and greedy. There is the risk of rejection.

A way to overcome your discomfort is to have a comfortable reason for reaching out to your targets. Instead of asking for business, you can offer something in one of the five categories of "value-in-advance."

Offer to provide some education. Conduct a complimentary seminar. Send an article that you have written.

Offer some entertainment. Invite someone to lunch or dinner. Invite people to participate in activities you enjoy.

Offer to introduce some of your contacts to each other. Look at your target list and identify the individuals who would benefit from meeting each other.

Take a leadership role. For example, volunteer for an assignment in your target's organization. You may have targets who would appreciate your being of service to causes they support.

Inspire your targets. In Chapter 4, we defined inspiration as the ability to instill self-confidence. We gave examples of how to be inspirational. People crave inspiration in their lives. The more you can inspire your targets, the more they will appreciate you and welcome your efforts to communicate with them.

By giving "value-in-advance" you are not directly asking for business and therefore, less likely to feel needy, pushy or greedy. Conversely, you will feel proud to reach out to your targets when you genuinely believe in the value you offer. When your targets perceive your offer as valuable, they are more likely to be receptive, and so the risk of rejection is minimized.

Effectiveness

In addition to reducing your embarrassment, "value-in-advance" is an effective strategy for motivating targets to hire you. We said earlier that your targets hire people they see as compatible and capable. Giving "value-in-advance" helps communicate compatibility and capability.

When you give a speech, you have an opportunity to reveal positive personal traits such as knowledge and expertise. Through your body language and your voice you can reveal qualities such as your energy, enthusiasm, confidence, and other positive personal traits that we described in Chapter 4.

These are qualities that you might otherwise feel awkward discussing. It sounds funny to say, "I'm smart. I'm energetic." But, when you speak in public, these qualities can be revealed. In Skill Module 1, we provide many tips on how to reveal these traits through public speaking.

Entertainment helps you communicate compatibility. Doing fun things such as golf, tennis, or dining out with your targets helps you build rapport and reveal positive personal qualities.

Introducing quality people to each other communicates compatibility and capability. It demonstrates that you know quality people. And, as those people interact with each other, it strengthens their emotional connection to you.

There is no question that taking on a leadership role communicates compatibility and capability. When your targets see you in a position of authority, it communicates capability. Your leadership role may not have anything to do with your practice area. For example, the task of helping plan a fund-raising dinner may have nothing to do with what you do for a living. However, many of the qualities that are needed in leadership are the same as those required for your profession. You need to be organized, persistent, and energetic. When your targets see you as a capable leader, it is logical for them to assume that you are also capable in your line of work.

Being inspirational is an effective way of revealing positive personal qualities. It can reveal qualities such as compassion, empathy, good communication skills, and knowledge.

Other Benefits of "Value-in-Advance"

So far, we have described two main reasons why "value-in-advance" helps you sell in your comfort zone: valid reasons to communicate with your targets, and the ability to communicate the benefits you offer. There are other reasons why "value-in-advance" helps you sell in your comfort zone. In Chapter 7, you will see how "value-in-advance" helps you reveal your interest in doing business. In Chapter 8, you will see examples of how "value-in-advance" helps you comfortably meet new people. And, in Chapter 9, we show you how to use "value-in-advance" to stay in touch with your targets.

The Obstacles to "Value-in-Advance"

As with other selling strategies, there are obstacles to giving "value-in-advance." Here are some common obstacles and suggestions for overcoming them.

The Fear of Public Speaking

Many people are uncomfortable with the thought of public speaking. The thought of getting up in front of an audience can be terrifying, especially if you don't have much practice.

In Skill Module 1, we give you several tips for overcoming your fear of public speaking. However, we feel it worth mentioning now that our philosophy for overcoming your fear of speaking is based on writing quality content. The fear of public speaking comes from the fear being embarrassed in front of people. When you develop content that you are proud of, you are less likely to feel embarrassed when you present it.

In Skill Module 1, we will show you how to write speeches of which you can be proud. We also give you some tips on how to present yourself effectively. Once you are confident that your speech will be well-received, you will feel less afraid of embarrassment.

Too Many Seminars

Many people say that they don't like the idea of conducting seminars because there are already too many competitors that do them. However, we believe that this is self-defeating thinking. Even if your competitors are actively giving seminars, it is unlikely that your targets have had their fill of quality speakers and programs. If your competitors are doing seminars, it is because there is a good reason. By refraining from doing seminars, you are allowing them to own that territory.

▼
Don't let your competition own the seminar territory.

Lack of Time

An obstacle for both speaking and writing is that they can require a lot of time. If you are busy, you may feel reluctant to pursue these tasks unless you are confident that they will be a wise investment of time. In Skill Modules 1, 2, and 3, we provide valuable tips for maximizing your success.

Lack of time is also an obstacle for leadership. Volunteering for committees can be time consuming. However, you need to consider the potential rewards. Many of our clients have become active in the trade groups of their clients and referral sources. In time, some of them went on to chair committees. One of our clients, who got referrals from lawyers, became president of his local bar association and generated hundreds of thousands of dollars in business.

In Chapters 5 and 8, we discuss strategies for selecting good targets to use your time wisely. In Skill Module 8, we give you tips for freeing up time.

> Use your time wisely by selecting well-targeted organizations.

The Risk of Making Introductions

Many people are afraid to make introductions because of the possibility that the people you introduce may not get along. Or worse, they may do a deal that goes badly. It is important that when you make an introduction, you are proud of the people you are introducing. Also, you don't need to make warranties. Rather, you should state that you are introducing people with the understanding that they get to know each other and decide for themselves if they feel comfortable working together.

> When you make introductions, select people you are proud of.

Discomfort with Entertainment

Many people are reluctant to blend business and entertainment. You many not enjoy social interaction. It may feel awkward or insincere. You may be concerned that your targets will find it manipulative. And, you may not be confident that it justifies the cost. Here are some tips for overcoming your discomfort with entertainment.

1. Do things that you enjoy.
2. Get people to talk about themselves.
3. Reveal your interest in doing business.
4. Use entertainment when appropriate.
5. Make a cost-benefit analysis.

Do Things That You Enjoy

We always recommend that you blend your business entertainment with the activities you enjoy. We have had many clients who have thought of themselves as social introverts but who have effectively used their hobbies and interests as a vehicle for entertaining their valued contacts.

We had a client who was an avid fisherman who took his business contacts on fishing trips. We had a client who used her love of playing the harp to invite prospects and clients to harp concerts in her home. We had a client who was passionate about wines and invited his contacts to local restaurants to sample wines and listen to wine-tasting experts.

We have had many clients on the boards of symphony orchestras, museums and theatres who have hosted special gatherings for their business contacts. Many of our clients who have children involved in school sporting activities have invited the parents of their children's teammates to barbecues as a way of bonding with the other parents.

The authors of this book love giving parties. One of our parties was in an art gallery. At one point during the party, guests were furnished with laser tag pistols. It was fascinating to see successful lawyers, doctors, accountants, and other professionals running around and hiding behind sculptures like little kids shooting their laser tag pistols at each other. The more fun or interesting your idea, the more people will be likely to attend, remember, and appreciate your invitation.

Your entertainment idea doesn't have to be a hobby or a passion. You may think of a creative idea that people would enjoy. One of our clients hired a famous dessert chef to give a presentation on chocolate desserts at a local cooking school. We had another client who asked a friend who was an authority on "Ancient Spice Routes in the Middle East" to give a lecture on a recent excavation that he had led. Over two hundred people came to hear the presentation. Not only was the evening a success, our client developed a lot of new business.

> ▼
> 🖎 Comfort zone task—Make a list of fun activities you would like to share with your targets.

You do not need the personality of an outgoing socialite to entertain. Once you learn that selling can be fun, you are more likely to feel enthusiastic about using entertainment in the sales process.

Get People to Talk about Themselves

The question comes up frequently, "When you entertain someone for business (for example, when you take someone to lunch) what do you talk about?" A good technique is to get your contacts talking about themselves. Given the chance, most people love to talk about themselves. You simply have to develop the skill of asking good questions.

You are not required to ask people for business. You don't have to boast about your service. Don't push yourself to sell. Your primary goal in entertaining people is to build rapport and trust. This not only takes the pressure off of you to be a good conversationalist, but it can actually be a more effective strategy for building rapport and trust.

Many years ago, Dale Carnegie, a famous author and teacher, inspired millions in his book "How to Win Friends and Influence People." (Simon & Schuster, Inc., 1981). Carnegie frequently made the point that becoming genuinely interested in other people is the most effective technique for building rapport. He says, "You can make more friends in two months by becoming interested in other people than you can in two years by trying to get other people interested in you."

The key is "genuine" interest. Don't try to feign interest. That will only feel manipulative and insincere. And, people can often see through a veiled attempt at interest. Find something about the person that genuinely interests you. Then, the interaction will be enjoyable for both of you.

Reveal Your Interest in Doing Business

Another question that often arises is, "How do you use entertainment without the risk of either feeling or appearing to be insincere?" You may have friends who are in a position to help you generate business. For example, you may know people who work for companies that need your services. But, there is the risk that approaching your friends may inadvertently damage your friendship. Some of your friends might think that you were only using them to get business.

The solution is to reveal your intentions to do business. You explain that there is a business component to your relationship. You might say something along the lines of: "I would like to invite you to lunch to talk about business." There are other effective techniques for revealing your interest in doing business that we discuss in Chapter 7 that will minimize the risk of your appearing insincere.

Use Entertainment When Appropriate

While entertainment is a highly common and absolutely appropriate technique for generating business, not everyone thinks it is appropriate. Some people are annoyed by vendors offering to take them to lunch. We had a client who said that one of his clients made it clear that he only wanted good work and no entertainment.

Some businesses actually prohibit entertainment by vendors. They don't want their employees selecting vendors because of personal benefit.

One solution to this obstacle is to not use entertainment for people who don't approve of it. Instead, look for people who are open to it. And, for those people who don't want to be entertained, find some other method of value to offer that they would appreciate. Many companies like seminars because of their educational value.

Make a Cost-Benefit Analysis

Of course, as with other forms of "value-in-advance," entertainment requires time and expense. So, you want to maximize its value to you. Here are some pros and cons of business entertainment methods.

Breakfast is a relatively quick and easy method to get to know someone, and you can get back to your office early so that the meal doesn't interfere with your day. Lunches are probably the most popular, because most people have lunch. But, a drawback of lunches is that they can take time out of the middle of the day.

Dinners are more expensive and time consuming, especially since you may be inviting spouses and dining at nice restaurants. But, with important targets, it may be worth the expense. One way to keep the dinner cost down is to entertain at home. An additional benefit of home entertainment is that it is more personal. You can reveal more about who you are in your home environment. People coming to your home can see your photographs, meet your family, and see your home. In this way, they can get a clearer sense of who you are and feel more connected to you.

Hosting large events can be a highly economical way to entertain. As you add people to your events, your cost per person often goes down. An added benefit of parties is that your contacts can meet each other. A drawback is that they may be difficult to plan. You have to select a venue and find a time when most people can attend.

Conclusion to "Value-in-Advance"

"Value-in-advance" is a proven method for safely and effectively communicating the value you offer through your deeds or actions. It gives you a valid reason to call your targets and it communicates the benefits you offer. Rather than merely saying that you offer value, it proves it. People can experience first-hand what it is like to work with you before they hire you.

2. Your Dialogue

Your dialogue is the second medium for communicating value. As with "value-in-advance," your dialogue can help you sell in your comfort zone. It can give you valid reasons for communicating with your targets and it can communicate the benefits you offer.

In Chapter 7, we show you how to use dialogue to develop valid reasons for communicating with your targets. In this chapter, we focus on dialogue that communicates benefits.

We focus on five methods of dialogue that help sell in your comfort zone. These are:

1. Describe your methodology.
2. Share your experiences.
3. Ask insightful questions.
4. Describe the obstacles your prospects are facing.
5. Quote fees in relation to benefits.

Describe Your Systems

One method of dialogue is to describe your systems that we outlined in Chapter 4—your guiding principles, policies and procedures, staff, training, and technology. An example we gave was the 24-hour call-back rule. As a way of instilling confidence, you could explain this rule. Instead simply saying that you are responsive, it feels less like bragging, and is more convincing to say that you have a rule that all calls are returned within a 24-hour period.

Share Your Experiences

Another method of dialogue is to give examples of experiences in which you helped other clients. However, make sure that you don't reveal confidential client information. Even the name of your client may be confidential in certain circumstances. Examples are more effective in revealing your experience than simply stating that you have experience. People are engaged by stories, and they create greater confidence in your skill.

We recommend that you spend some time thinking about situations in which you helped your clients. This will help you to be prepared when prospects have problems you have experience fixing. Instead of saying, "I have experience with that," you will have concrete examples of how you helped someone with a similar problem.

▼

🖎 Comfort zone task—Accumulate stories about how you have helped clients solve problems.

Ask Insightful Questions

Asking insightful questions is a third method of dialogue. When you are meeting with a prospect, instead of telling them how knowledgeable you are and how much experience you have, ask questions that reveal your in-depth understanding of their problems. Insightful questions are more effective in revealing your knowledge than boasting about it. After they answer your questions, then you can give your opinion about how you would solve their problems.

Describe the Obstacles Your Prospects Are Facing

It is helpful to your prospects to explain the obstacles they are facing. It reveals an in-depth knowledge of their situations. It demonstrates empathy. It gives them hope that solutions are available. And, it positions you as someone who can assist them.

Quote Fees in Relation to Benefits

Quoting fees is another part of your dialogue. When you quote fees, it is important to quote them in relation to the benefits that you offer. If people are going to spend money, they have to feel confident that they will receive sufficient benefits. So, when you quote your fees, don't give your rates in a vacuum. Remember to precede your fees with a reminder of the benefits you offer. If possible, describe the monetary benefits your clients can expect. Explain how much you can help your prospects either earn or save. And, discuss the non-monetary benefits, which are your systems and any added-benefits you regularly offer. Discuss your methodologies and resources. And, if possible, describe how your services are differentiated from the competition.

Remember that value is a ratio of benefits to fees. The more benefits that you describe, the more likely your prospects will perceive to be getting a good deal.

3. Your Documents

The third medium for communicating value is your documents, including your brochure, Web site, bios, published articles, and newsletters. These techniques will be discussed at length in *Skill Module 4: Tips for documenting the value you offer.*

Conclusion

The purpose of this chapter was to help you identify strategies for communicating value to your targets. There are three mediums of communication: your deeds, your dialogue, and your documents. In using these three mediums, you can develop strategies that will increase your expectations of safety and effectiveness.

Reveal Your Interest in Doing Business 7

The sooner you reveal
Your intent to do a deal.
The truth you won't conceal
And the better you will feel.

REVEALING YOUR INTEREST IN DOING BUSINESS is another important strategy for selling in your comfort zone. This refers to the process of letting people know what kind of a relationship you are trying to establish. This is not always a required step in the selling process. In some cases, your contacts already know that you are interested in doing business. When a prospect approaches you for assistance, and you make a proposal to offer your services, then, obviously, your objectives are clear. But, there will be many circumstances in which it will be beneficial, even necessary, to reveal your interest in doing business.

The Reasons for Revealing Your Interest in Doing Business

A lot of people you know may simply not make the connection that you are interested in doing business with them. Maybe you know people in an organization such as the PTA or an activity, such as a baseball league. Your contacts may think of you as a friend or social acquaintance, but not as a business contact. Perhaps you have contacts who haven't yet perceived a need for someone with your skills. It just never crosses their minds that you could be doing business.

When you meet new people, depending upon the circumstances in which you meet, it may not be clear that you could be doing work for them. You may meet someone at a social event and the topic of what you do for a living may not come up. In these cases, you need appropriate ways of making known your interest in doing business.

Different Communication Approaches

There are many ways of revealing your interest in doing business. Your style can range from discreet to direct. There is no one style that will be appropriate for every circumstance.

Some people are very blunt about revealing their interest in doing business. For example, we have known people who would come right out and say, "I want your business." Or, they'd ask, "Why haven't you sent me any work!?" They feel no compunction about being totally upfront.

However, you may not feel comfortable being direct. One of our clients said, "I don't like the hard-sell approach. I don't want to sound like I am making a sales pitch. My style is to take people to lunch or a ball game, and to be friendly. Gradually, they learn what I do and, if they want to, they can hire me."

The "Value-in-Advance" Approach

This client is using the technique of giving value in advance as we described in Chapter 6 to reveal his interest in doing business. He entertains his contacts and focuses on building a social relationship. It is a highly common technique and often very effective.

When you give "value-in-advance," your interest in doing business is often implicit. For example, when you offer to give a speech on a business-related topic, most people will understand that your goal is to develop business. You probably don't have to state the obvious: "I am giving this speech because I hope that you hire me."

The same can be said with other types of "value-in-advance." When you entertain business contacts, most people understand that lunches, dinners, and other types of entertainment are intended for getting work. When you send a newsletter, a reprint of an article, or even when you offer to take a leadership role in the trade organizations of your clients, your intentions are often implicitly understood.

You May Need to Be More Direct

However, there may be times when "value-in-advance" is insufficient to communicate your interest in doing business. We had a client who spent several years volunteering his time in non-profit organizations, giving value by participating on committees and boards. In the process, he developed wonderful friendships with many of his fellow members. Many of these members were professionals and business people who could have used our client's services and made referrals. But, our client was reluctant to reveal his interest in doing business, and his fellow members never became clients or referral sources.

In fact, he was astounded to discover that some of his fellow members had been sending work to other service providers that he could have handled. These service providers weren't even members of the organization. Later, a few of his fellow members told him, "Had I known that you did this sort of thing, I would have sent it to you." Our client had made the error of being too discreet. Realizing his mistake, we helped him change his philosophy and develop comfortable ways of more clearly revealing his interest in doing business. In a matter of months, he started generating referrals.

There are many ways of being more direct in how you reveal your interest in doing business. Here are some examples of different approaches.

> ▼
> The direct approach is often the quickest and most sincere.

Talk about Your Work

One technique is to talk about your work during conversations with your contacts. At a cocktail party or over dinner, instead of talking about only personal topics, when you see an opportunity you might say something such as, "That reminds me of a situation at work." Then, you have the opportunity to talk about issues at work that position you as knowledgeable and experienced in your field.

One opportunity that is often overlooked is when friends ask you the question, "How are you?" Instead of saying "fine," and leaving it at that, you could go on to say, "In fact, there are some interesting legal issues I am working on." This opens the door to discuss how you help your clients.

Just Say What Is on Your Mind

You may have contacts with whom it would be appropriate to openly discuss your interest in doing business. You might feel comfortable simply saying to a contact, "We should look for ways to work together." Or, "I would love to have an opportunity to work with you."

One client volunteered for the PTA at his children's school. Through his efforts, he developed a friendship with a qualified target. They were always friendly when they saw each other at PTA meetings. But, our client didn't know how to make the conversion to a business relationship. So, we recommended that he call the contact and say, "All of these years that we have known each other, we have never discussed the possibility of our doing business. I'd like to talk with you about how we could do business together." His contact said, "Absolutely." They scheduled lunch and ultimately referred business to each other.

Ask for Permission to Bring up the Subject

With some people, you may be able to discuss the issue of doing business by asking for permission to raise a subject. One of our clients used this technique effectively by taking a friend to lunch, and discussing their families and other personal interests. And then, he would say, "I'd like your permission to change the subject. It occurs to me that you and I are in businesses that may be mutually beneficial. May I bring up a subject concerning business to see if it is worth pursuing?"

Reveal Your Feelings

Another technique involves revealing your feelings about the idea of doing business. In talking with a contact, you might say, "There is a subject that I have been meaning to bring up with you but I have felt a little reluctant because I am concerned that you would feel as if I am imposing on you. I am bringing this up with the understanding that if you don't think that it is a good idea, don't worry about it. You have a company that we could be providing services for. And, I would like to explore how we might do that."

By expressing your concern about imposing on your friends, you take away the risk of appearing manipulative or of being an imposition. Because this technique involves revealing your honest feelings, we call it "The Full-Disclosure Technique."

Ask about the Approval Procedures

An effective technique for revealing your desire to do business is to ask about your contacts approval process. We had a client who invited his prospects to a series of complimentary educational seminars as a way of generating business. He had a tremendous turn-out. There were several decision-makers from qualified targets that attended. But, our client typically didn't follow up after the seminars to reveal his interest in doing business. Our client was concerned about the appearance being "diplomatic." He didn't want to be perceived as too pushy or needy by the prospects. He felt that if someone wanted his services, they knew what he did and they would call. Unfortunately, while some of his prospects said that they would call him to use his services, they never did.

We suggested the idea that he follow-up with each person who had attended the meetings to thank them for coming and to find out their procedures for getting on their approved vendor lists. He saw the value of trying this approach and so he experimented with calling each prospect to find out their approval procedures. Sometimes there were formal applications and processes. And other times he simply needed to go in and visit with them in person. He got several new clients directly as a result of this calling effort. This was a comfortable way of revealing his interest in doing business that directly led to new clients.

Ask for Advice

A variation of this technique is to ask your contacts for their advice about how to get approved to do business with their companies. In this way you are not appearing overly pushy. You are merely asking for advice.

We had a client who had a friend that worked for a company he wanted to do business with. His friend wasn't in a position of hiring authority, but he felt reluctant to ask his friend to introduce him to the decision-makers. So, instead, he asked his friend for advice on how to meet the decision-makers. He said, "I feel uncomfortable asking you to make this introduction. But, since you work there, perhaps you can give me some advice on how I might go about meeting the right people." His friend came up with a good idea. He said, "The next time you are in the area, stop by to visit and I will introduce you."

Talk about Your Colleagues

We have had clients who were uncomfortable revealing their interest in doing business because it seemed too self-promotional. But, they were happy to talk about their colleagues. If you have partners and you are proud of the work that they do, an effective technique for revealing your interest in doing business is to talk about the services that they provide.

Explain your reasons for socializing

Much of selling involves social activities such as taking people to lunch, dinner, or ballgames. It is important to become friendly with your targets when you are attempting to develop business. People do business with people they like.

But, you may have targets with whom you don't want to become close friends. If you are not clear in revealing your true intentions, there is the risk of your contacts getting the wrong impression. The way to avoid this risk is to reveal your interest early in the relationship-building process. You might say something to the effect of, "I'd like to suggest that we get together for lunch to discuss the possibility of doing business." Honestly revealing your intentions early makes it known from the outset that there is a business component to the relationship.

Being direct often feels more honest and sincere

Interestingly, many people who are initially uncomfortable with selling prefer being candid about their intentions to do business. You might think that a person who is uncomfortable with selling would prefer a more discreet approach. But actually, people who don't like selling often say that the more direct approach seems more honest and sincere.

Conclusion

There are many different ways of appropriately and accurately revealing your interest in doing business. We recommend that you now look at your list of targets and decide if you have contacts that you would feel comfortable approaching using one of the above techniques.

Find Comfortable Techniques for Meeting New People

8

Even though you have some contacts
Understanding what you do
But the ones who want to hire you
Are a disappointing few,
Then you need to meet new contacts
And to minimize the chore
You should look for concentrations.
You'll work less and you'll meet more.

ANOTHER IMPORTANT REQUIREMENT for staying in your comfort zone is to find comfortable techniques for meeting new people. Up to this point, we have discussed methods of selling to people who you already know. However, your base of existing contacts may not be large enough to sustain an effective selling effort. To be successful, you will need to meet new people.

The Obstacles to Meeting New People

Before discussing comfortable techniques for meeting new people, let's briefly review the obstacles. The obstacles can be divided into two categories: *external* and *internal.*

External Obstacles
External obstacles are barriers over which you have little control. For example, the people that you would like to meet may

be difficult to reach. They may be busy. Or, they may be wary about meeting strangers. Imagine how *you* feel when strangers call you to sell something. Chances are that you put up your guard. You don't want to be annoyed and have your time wasted by salespeople who you don't know or trust.

Another external obstacle is the expense involved in meeting new people. As you will see, you may want to join organizations, or produce seminars. These things cost money. Advertising is another way of generating new contacts. And although we don't discuss advertising in this book because it is technically not a part of the selling process and too large in scope for us to handle in a single book, advertising can be extremely expensive. Fortunately, there are many lower cost ways of meeting people that we will discuss.

Internal Obstacles

Internal obstacles are your feelings, beliefs, and old habits that restrict your ability to meet new people. For example, the fear of rejection is a common obstacle. Nobody we know, not even extroverts, is comfortable with rejection.

Your lifestyle may be an obstacle, particularly if you are shy or introverted. Unlike extroverts, who naturally seek out opportunities to meet new people, you may enjoy staying at home or in the office.

Finally, you may have preconceived ideas about methods for meeting new people. You may only be familiar with traditional techniques that don't fall within your comfort zone. One well-known traditional technique is "working a room."

Working a room is the technique of going to activities and walking up to strangers to introduce yourself. Although many people use this technique effectively, most of the people we work with find it to be distasteful and inefficient.

We are not saying that you should completely rule out working a room. In fact, if you can learn to overcome your discomfort with this technique, it can be extremely useful. In Skill Module 6, we give you several tips for increasing your comfort and effectiveness with this method. However, if you are currently uncomfortable with this technique, there are several alternative methods that may fall within your current comfort zone.

Review Target Criteria from Chapter 5

The first step in meeting new people is to be aware of the types of targets you are interested in meeting. Begin by reviewing the two comfort criteria we described in Chapter 5. These criteria are targets which are likely to lead to new business, and targets you like.

Become Aware of Your Target Demographics

You should also know your targets' demographics, including industry, income, number of employees, and location. The more you know about your targets' demographics, the easier it will be to find and meet them. For example, if you want to meet prospects or referral sources in a particular industry, you could find a list of all of the trade groups that support that industry and attend their meetings.

One way to become aware of the demographics of your ideal targets is to look for similarities among your existing and past clients and referral sources. Another technique for becoming aware of demographics is to envision what types of people benefit from and can afford your services.

Three Strategies for Finding and Meeting Your Targets

Once you are clear about the types of targets you are interested in meeting, the next step is to find and meet them. Here are three safe and effective strategies for finding and meeting your targets:

1. Encourage introductions from the people you know.
2. Reach out through organizations.
3. Reach out through public relations.

1. Encourage Introductions

One strategy is to encourage your contacts to introduce you to the people they know. Both you and your targets are more likely to feel comfortable knowing that you have a mutual contact and that you have been recommended.

Identify Your Allies

Begin by reviewing the list of contacts that we helped you create in Chapter 5. In Chapter 5, we described several categories of people such as clients, colleagues, advisors, friends, and family, who may have the ability to make introductions. From this list, select the people who you believe to be your allies—people who are willing to make introductions.

Unfortunately, not everyone in a position to help you is going to be an ally. Look for the people who are.

Consider the people you know who would financially benefit from your bringing in new business. For example, your partners or supervisor

Figure 5

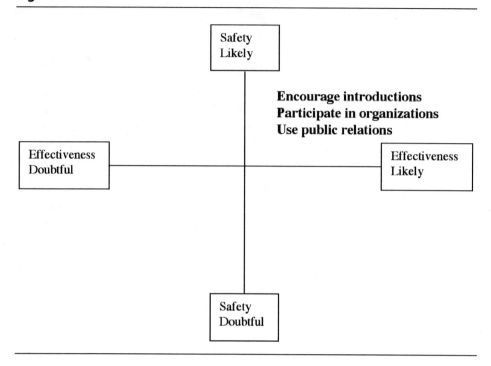

might be potential allies. We had a client who was being encouraged by her boss to bring in new clients. But, she didn't know many people. As it turns out, her boss had a lot of quality contacts who he wasn't pursuing for business because he didn't have the time. We suggested that she ask him if he would feel comfortable reviewing his rolodex and picking out names of people that he thought she should meet. He agreed and she came away with over two dozen names of prospects and potential referral sources to call.

Consider the people who have benefited from your services in the past. You may have clients who appreciate the value you have given them and who would be willing to introduce you to their competitors and/or advisors.

> ✍ Comfort zone task—Make a list of people you know who are willing and able to make introductions.

Consider your friends and family who may want to see you succeed. We have many clients who have gotten business because a friend or family member introduced them to a quality target.

Find the Right Message

Once you have identified the people who you believe are both willing and able to help you, the next step is to decide how to encourage your contacts to make introductions. You don't want to risk harming relationships. But, you *do* what to reveal your interest in meeting people. Otherwise, it may never occur to your contacts that you want to meet new people.

Examples of direct techniques

Sometimes the direct approach works best to get introductions. Phrase your request in way that makes your contact feel comfortable. Avoid putting them on the spot. Explain to your contacts that you are interested in meeting new people and ask if they would feel comfortable introducing you to their contacts. Tell them not to feel obligated to make the introduction. As discussed earlier, you could use "full disclosure" and say that you don't want to put your contacts in an awkward position. If they feel comfortable, however, you would appreciate the introduction.

▼

✍ Comfort zone task—Create comfortable dialogue for encouraging introductions.

Another direct technique is to ask your contacts to think of organizations in which you could meet qualified targets. You may have contacts involved in Rotary clubs, chambers of commerce, trade or professional groups, or other organizations that would be fertile environments for meeting new people. Ask your contacts if they would feel comfortable inviting you as their guest to attend a meeting.

Examples of indirect techniques

If you are uncomfortable with being direct with your contacts, then you may be able to use an indirect technique. One indirect technique is to introduce your targets to people they would like to meet. Making introductions often creates "introductions receivable." When you introduce two people to each other, they may be more inclined to reciprocate by introducing you to their contacts.

▼

✍ Comfort zone task—Create "Introductions Receivable," by introducing the people you know to each other.

Another effective indirect technique for meeting people through your contacts is to do seminars. If you have contacts that work at companies, you may want to meet their colleagues. Conducting on-site seminars provides you an opportunity to meet these people.

2. Reach Out Through Organizations

Another way of meeting new people is through organizations. There are many types of organizations that may facilitate your selling effort. There are trade groups, professional associations, charities, community-based organizations, political action groups, networking groups, discussion groups, and clubs.

The right organizations can provide a comfortable and even enjoyable environment for meeting new qualified targets. Also, organizations can provide a forum for building trust and rapport with your targets.

Four Characteristics of Quality Organizations

In determining which organizations to participate in, here are some characteristics to look for:

1. A high concentration of qualified targets
2. A purpose that you support
3. Practical meeting locations
4. Meaningful communication opportunities

1. A High Concentration of Qualified Targets

If your goal is business development, research the organization to determine if it attracts quality targets before you join. Recall the two targeting criteria we gave you in Chapter 5: the potential to lead to new business, and likeability.

The first criterion looks for targets that have the potential to lead to new business, including quality prospects, quality referral sources, and quality resources.

Quality *prospects* are people that have the need, authority, and financial capacity to hire you. Quality *referral sources* are people who know your ideal prospects and have the credibility in the minds of their contacts to recommend you. Quality *resources* are people who can provide entrée to your ideal prospects and referral sources through organizations and other opportunities.

Trade and professional groups

If you have clients and referral sources that are concentrated in a particular profession, then a trade or professional group would be a good place for you to join. Most industries and professions have trade or professional groups that provide support in the form of education, lobbying, and networking. Trade and professional groups can bring you into direct contact with your ideal targets and give you the ability to bond and build credibility with them through your participation in their activities.

However, some trade and professional groups do not permit members from outside of their industries. If membership isn't an option, then perhaps you can offer to speak at their programs, write articles for their publications, or sponsor some of their events as a way of communicating with the members.

If you can get business from people within your own profession it makes sense to join your professional trade associations. One of our clients, a lawyer who got referrals from other lawyers, joined the board of a local bar association and in two years became chair of his section. The visibility from that position has led to his generating over $600,000 per year in new business.

The second criterion is to look for people who you like. Look for people with whom you share things in common such as interests, values and beliefs. The more things you share in common, the more intellectually and emotionally connected you will feel, and the more comfortable you will be in pursuing them.

Personal interest groups

You may want to look for groups that share your interests. We have clients with a wide range of hobbies, such as wine collectors, photographers, computer buffs, and sports enthusiasts, who have found clubs that support their interests. These groups are enjoyable and provide entrée to people with similar interests who may also be prospects and referral sources.

Peer-based groups

In considering which organization to join, consider ones that bring you in touch with your peers. Depending upon your profession, age, gender, political views, values, economic status, and ethnicity you may have certain comfort criteria.

People in a particular profession often feel comfortable spending time together because they speak a similar language and share encounter similar work-related experiences. So they find organizations in their professions that cater to their professional needs.

People of a similar age often feel connected. There are often organizations within professions or charities that support networking among certain age groups.

Many of our clients who are women find that women's organizations are a comfortable place to network. One of our clients said that she thought the world was a man's club. A turning point in her career was identifying a women's group where she met dozens of quality referral sources.

If you are a member of a particular ethnic group, you may feel comfortable finding organizations that bring together people with similar ethnic backgrounds. If you are a member of a minority there are many organizations that support doing business with minorities.

Research the membership

Before joining or taking an active role in an organization, you should always do research to find out as much as possible about its membership. Find out who is on the board of directors. Go to a few meetings and see who attends. Often, organizations will permit potential members to attend a few meetings before joining. Sometimes you can get someone you know who is already a member to invite you as a guest.

2. A Purpose That You Support

Make sure that you support the purpose of the organization you join. If you are not enthusiastic about the purpose of the organization, you won't feel comfortable attending their activities.

Charities and other non-profits

We know many people who participate in charities and community-based organizations that raise money for a wide range of worthy causes such as feeding the homeless, helping children who live in difficult neighborhoods, and curing diseases. In addition to being emotionally fulfilling, they can also be fertile environments for meeting potential clients and referral sources. A lot of successful business people support and participate in charities. Getting active can be a comfortable way to meet and get to know them.

Networking groups

Many organizations are created specifically for the purpose of meeting people that can help you develop new business. Some of these groups are large and have a national or international presence. Others are local. The advantage of a networking group is that the purpose of meeting people is disclosed and everyone who is a member knows that networking is not only accepted, it is expected. So, you don't have to feel embarrassed about your reasons for being there.

3. Practical Meeting Locations

Consider how far away the meetings are. Some groups may meet locally. National organizations may have meetings around the country. Find an organization that allows you to stay within your travel budget. In making this analysis, also factor the business development potential. It may be worth a few thousand dollars in travel expenses if you can generate more than that in fees from a potential new client.

4. Meaningful Communication Opportunities

In deciding which organizations to join, look for groups that provide comfortable opportunities for communicating with their members. Different organizations provide various communication opportunities.

Committees

Many organizations have committees that you can join. Taking a leadership role is an effective way of meeting your committee members and bonding with them in a non-threatening environment. You can work together for the common good of the organization and in the process reveal a lot about the value that you offer. People choose to do business with people they know and trust. As you work together, people will often learn about what you do and develop a sense of your ability.

Just make sure that you don't bite off more than you can chew. It is very easy to get overwhelmed with organization responsibilities. If you agree to do more than is possible, it could easily damage your credibility.

Networking activities

Many organizations, even if they are not networking groups, provide networking opportunities. They may hold events that are often a combination of a speaker and dinner. These programs allow you to meet people at a reception before or after the main event, or at the tables where you are seated.

Even philanthropic organizations often have a networking component. We have been active in many charities that have industry groups that give their contributors the opportunity to network with each other. But, be careful. Some philanthropic organizations may have policies that discourage aggressive solicitation. Even so, they give you the ability to meet quality people, and this often indirectly results in developing new business.

Public speaking

Many organizations have programs in which you could offer to speak at their educational programs as a way of meeting their members. We will discuss this more in our discussion on public relations and in Skill Module 3.

Publishing articles

Many organizations have newsletters or magazines for which you can write articles. These publications may be looking for material to publish. If you enjoy writing, this can be an effective way of gaining exposure and building credibility. We give you more information about writing and publishing articles in Skill Module 3.

How to Find the Right Organizations

Once you are aware of the characteristics that you should be looking for, the next step is to find the organizations that have these characteristics.

Do Research

The easiest way to find organizations is to ask people you know. Ask your clients if they participate in or are aware of any good organizations for meeting people. If your clients are involved in a particular organization, then there is a good chance that there are members who are quality prospects.

> ▼
> ✎ Comfort zone task—Ask your clients, colleagues, and other allies what organizations they're in.

Ask your friends and everyone else you know what groups they belong to. A lot of people you know may be involved in non-profit groups, business groups, or interest groups. If some you know can invite you to attend an organization meeting, then you will probably feel more comfortable participating because you have a host.

Another technique for finding quality organizations is to consider your clients' industries, and then look for the trade groups that represent those industries. Just about every industry has at least one trade group. As you become known in those trade groups, you may become established as the provider of choice.

> ▼
> ✎ Comfort zone task—Identify the trade groups of your clients and referral sources.

Be Persistent

It may take time to find the right organizations. And, it may not necessarily be easy. While there are a lot of potential organizations in the world, not all of them have the right mix of targets, or are geographically convenient, or cost effective. You have to be patient, but also persistent in your search for the right organization.

A lot of people are skeptical about their ability to find quality organizations. One client said he couldn't find a good organization to join. The truth was that he really hadn't tried very hard. He asked one of his clients if they were active in an organization and they weren't. So, he jumped to that conclusion that nobody he knew was aware of organizations. But, after many months of our prodding him, he found a group through his brother-in-law that was filled with potential targets, which ultimately led to a lot of business.

Create Your Own Organization

Consider starting your own organization. One client, who is an environmental engineer, created a small discussion group composed of people in different, but related, fields to discuss environmental issues. A lot of business was generated as a result of these get-togethers.

One of our clients loved literature, and started a book reading club. He brought together a collection of friends, clients, prospects, and referral sources who shared a mutual interest in books. Each month, he assigned a book to read which would be discussed. The members of the club enjoyed the meetings, built close friendships, and did business with each other.

Two consultants in California came up with the brilliant idea of creating an organization that would attract their ideal prospects and referral sources. They were interested in targeting people in the field of mergers and acquisitions, banking and finance. They formed a group called the Professional's Networking Group or PNG. It was designed to attract other professionals who wanted to build their sphere of contacts. The organization blossomed, attracting hundreds of quality targets from around the state for the founders to meet and interact with on a regular basis.

Keep Looking for Additional Organizations

Once you find one or more organizations that really work for you, keep in mind that there may be a point of diminishing return over time. Eventually, you may meet and build relationships with all of the qualified targets. So, it may not be necessary to continue attending events. Or, your business may change and so will the types of targets you want to meet. Keep looking for other organizations that will bring you in touch with new qualified targets.

3. Reach Out Through Public Relations

Another effective method for meeting new people is public relations. Use public relations tactics to help you to meet people, such as getting articles published, getting quoted, doing public speaking, and implementing seminars.

Many companies hire publicists and public relations companies. However, hiring someone can be quite costly; especially since public relations is often a long-term process. It could take many years to get results. Fortunately, even if you are on a small budget, you can enjoy the benefits of public relations by learning how to do it yourself.

We give tips for implementing public relations techniques in Skill Modules 1, 2, and 3. Here is a brief summary:

Publish Articles

As mentioned earlier, an effective technique for meeting new people is to write articles and then get those articles published. Articles are an indirect way of meeting new people. There is no personal interaction. You are relying on people to see your articles and become motivated to call you. But, one of the great benefits of articles is that you can make reprints which can be used as mailers and handouts, and supplement your brochure. Another great benefit of articles is that when people see them it reinforces their perception of you as an expert.

The key to getting articles published is to call the editors of publications that are read by your target audience. If you have a topic that their readers find interesting, and you have a good article, then you have a shot at getting published. Refer to Skill Module 3 for tips on writing and publishing.

Communicate with the Media

Another way of gaining exposure and stimulating people to call you is to get quoted in the press or have articles written about you. This exposure gives you the benefit of third party endorsement. There is a perception that people who are quoted have been vetted by the media and determined to be experts. There are tips on getting media exposure in Skill Module 3.

Offer to Do Public Speaking

Public speaking is an effective way of gaining exposure and directly meeting people who need your services. Many organizations offer speaking opportunities.

Public speaking is one of the most effective business generation techniques because it can give you entrée to large numbers of people and position you as an authority. The key is to identify the groups that attract your targets and get in touch with the person in charge of finding speakers for programs. This may be a staff person or volunteer. You could even have an administrative person find the right person and then call to see if your topics would be of interest to their groups. Of course, a lot of professionals are uncomfortable with public speaking. There is the risk of rejection and embarrassment. We provide many tips on getting, making quality speeches, and overcoming your discomfort with public speaking in Skill Module 1.

Conduct Seminars

Another effective public relations technique for meeting new people is to conduct seminars. Conducting seminars is a comfortable technique of reaching out to strangers because they offer "value-in-advance." You can invite people by calling them on the phone or sending invitations via mail or email. If you don't have the time or desire to make the invitations yourself, the task can be delegated to an administrative person. If you have a large enough budget, you could even advertise. When people attend your seminars, you have the ability to meet them and build credibility by providing valuable information.

Seminars can be large, lengthy programs. Or they can be small and inexpensive. If you don't have a lot of experience conducting seminars, we recommend beginning with small events in which you invite a few good contacts and host them in your office. Because they are easier and less expensive, you are more likely to do them. And, after you gain practice with small seminars, you can experiment with larger programs.

A very practical and cost-effective way of conducting seminars is to do joint-venture seminars. Team up with one or more professionals who you don't compete with but who have clients with similar demographics. Then, each of you can invite a few of your contacts to the seminar and in that way, meet each others' contacts.

Of course, there are many obstacles to doing seminars. They can be time consuming and costly. It may be hard to come up with topics. However, all of these obstacles can be overcome and we provide many tips for conducting effective seminars in Skill Module 2.

Conclusion

Meeting new people is an important part of your selling effort. However, meeting new people can be uncomfortable. There are many risks. It can also be time consuming. To stay in your comfort zone, you have to find ways of meeting new people that give you a high expectation of safety and effectiveness.

We recommend that you begin by leveraging your existing contacts. Select people who have the ability and willingness to make introductions. Develop the appropriate dialogue so that you feel comfortable asking for introductions.

In addition, you can meet people through organizations. Make sure that you target organizations that have the right demographics and ample opportunities for communicating with members.

And finally, use public relations as a vehicle for meeting new people. Reach out to the media, offer to speak, and conduct seminars. Use techniques that give value and position you as an authority in your field.

Of course, there are obstacles to meeting new people. But, by planning your strategies, doing research, and taking appropriate action, you can safely and effectively build your base of contacts.

Develop Comfortable Systems to Stay in Touch

9

Stay in touch with your targets
And then you will find
When needs are perceived
You will be top-of-mind.

UP TO THIS POINT, we have discussed comfortable ways of identifying your best targets, communicating value to those targets, and meeting new, qualified targets. Now we focus on another important requirement of selling in your comfort zone: developing comfortable systems for staying in touch with your targets.

Reasons to Stay in Touch

A lot of people don't understand the importance of staying in touch. A common belief is "I have met my targets. They know what I do and if they need me they will call me." But, there are several fallacies with this philosophy.

It could take a long time for people to appreciate the value that you offer, and to develop trust in your ability to help them. Even if they appreciate and trust you, the timing may not be right.

As we pointed out in Chapter 5, you may have long-term targets. They may not have an immediate need for your services. They may not be at a stage at which they can

▼

It is important to maintain a consistent, positive presence in the minds of your targets.

afford your services. They may not have the authority right now to hire you. Or they may have pre-existing relationships with your competition. But, it is important to maintain a consistent and positive presence in their minds so that, should the timing be right, they will think of you.

The Obstacles to Staying in Touch

However, there are many obstacles to staying in touch. Here are a few:

The Fear of Appearing Pushy or Needy

A lot of people are uncomfortable with the idea of staying in touch because they are concerned about being perceived as pushy or needy. So, they hold off communicating with their targets. They often justify their decision to postpone with the belief that somehow it will feel more comfortable to call in the future. In reality, the longer you wait, the more difficult it usually becomes to re-open doors.

If you call people out of the blue who you haven't been in touch with for many years, they may find it strange that you are suddenly calling. And, you may find it more difficult to come up with a comfortable reason for calling. Even worse, with the passing of time you may forget about some of your contacts altogether. Many of our clients have acknowledged that over the years, their failure to stay in touch with their contacts resulted in many qualified targets slipping away.

The Obstacle of Limited Resources

As we have mentioned many times in this book, an obstacle to selling is limited time and money. It may seem difficult to find the time or money to stay in touch with all of your qualified contacts. This becomes more of a challenge as you meet more people. Fortunately, there are both practical and comfortable techniques for staying in touch.

Techniques for Staying in Touch

There are two main categories of techniques for staying in touch: *group outreach and individual outreach.*

Group Outreach

You can never be certain where business may come from. Our clients report getting business from a wide variety of sources, such as a next-door neighbor, an old friend they haven't heard from in years, even a past client that they thought was dissatisfied.

You may have a lot of contacts who are not primary targets and don't warrant your close attention. But, you don't want to lose touch with them either. So, it is imperative that you have the ability to stay in touch with everybody that has the potential to help you generate new business. This increases the likelihood of your targets thinking of you when the timing is right.

Maintain a mailing list (or contact database)

A mailing list or contact database is a cost-effective and manageable system for maintaining the names of all of your quality targets. It allows you to keep in a central location the names of everyone you have met, and will continue to meet in the future.

A quality mailing list gives you the ability to quickly communicate with all of your contacts and to track them as they move and grow in their careers. If you have something of value to send to your contacts such as a newsletter, a recently published article, or an invitation to an event, a mailing list gives you the ability to easily distribute it. It doesn't take much to maintain a significant presence with your targets. If you were to send a holiday card once a year, it would help to keep the door open.

Even if you can't think of anything right now to send to your contacts, a mailing list will at least prevent you from forgetting about them altogether. It gives you the ability to review your list of contacts from time to time to see if there is anyone that you could be reaching out to. And, if you develop ideas for communicating with contacts in the future, you will have compiled a comprehensive list of names of people to whom you can reach out.

We had a client who didn't have a mailing list. Then one day he was interviewed by a reporter from a national magazine and he wanted to send copies to all of his contacts. But, because he hadn't assembled a mailing list, he didn't have the ability to send it. So, per our direction he began the process of building a mailing list. He started compiling names of contacts that he had met over the 20 years he had been in business. It took a long time because he was busy and understaffed. Many of the addresses for his contacts were no longer good and had to be updated. Some contacts were hard to track. By the time he had compiled the list; the article was not as timely so he didn't send it out. Fortunately, he learned the lesson. He began to keep his mailing up-to-date and now when he has something to send out, it goes out immediately.

Mailing list maintenance improves selling awareness

One of the greatest benefits of keeping a mailing list is that it helps you to get in the habit of thinking about selling. You may recall the importance of developing greater selling awareness in Chapter 1. Building and maintaining a mailing list is a relatively easy and comfortable way of staying focused on selling. The process of asking for someone's business card, having that information added to your list, and tracking that person if letters or emails get returned, helps to reinforce your thinking about selling. You reinforce your selling awareness each time you review your list and consciously ask yourself whether or not a particular contact belongs on the list.

In time, this greater awareness of selling will help you notice more selling opportunities and become more comfortable with the overall process. Even if you are currently not planning to make selling an active part of your life, you should create and maintain a mailing list at minimum. So, when you are ready to step up your sales effort, you will have accumulated a quality list of people with whom to communicate.

Mailing list software

While some people are still content to keep the names of their contacts in a Rolodex, business card file, or address book, we recommend using mailing list software.

There are several mailing list software programs on the market. We recommend finding software that gives you the ability to categorize the industry each target is in. This will help you do selective outreach. For example, you may decide that you want to do a seminar for a particular group such as bankers or CPAs. If you have categorized your targets this way, you will quickly be able to find and communicate with everyone in these categories.

There may be other categories of information you would like to track. For example, you may want to look up contacts that are prospects or referral sources. You may want to track important dates, such as birthdays or anniversaries. Look for a mailing list that gives you the ability to create the categories that will help you do meaningful searches.

Also, you may want the ability to schedule follow-up dates. Contact databases give you the ability to calendar when you want to communicate with important contacts so that you don't forget to stay in touch.

Start inputting names

Once you have selected a mailing list program, we recommend you immediately start entering your contacts. If you don't have time yourself, then you may want to consider hiring someone to do it for you. But, don't procrastinate. Make this a priority.

You can use the mailing maintenance form in Exhibit B to assist you in the process of building your mailing list and keeping it up-to-date. Keep a stack of these forms at your fingertips.

Each time you meet someone new, or learn that someone has moved, or even decide to delete someone from your list, fill out the form. If you are

Exhibit B—Mailing List Maintenance Form

DATE: ___/___/___

☐ **ADD**   ☐ **EDIT**   ☐ **TRACK**   ☐ **DELETE**

TITLE:_____ NAME: _____ POSITION: _____

FIRM/COMPANY: _____

ADDRESS: _____SUITE: _____

CITY/STATE/ZIP: _____

INDUSTRY: _____ SOURCE (NAME): _____

BUSINESS PHONE: (_____) _____-_____

FAX #:   (_____) _____-_____   DATA ENTRY

HOME PHONE: (_____) _____-_____   BY:_____

CELL PHONE: (_____) _____-_____   DATE: _____/_____/_____

E-MAIL ADDRESS: _____

DATE: ___/___/___

☐ **ADD**   ☐ **EDIT**   ☐ **TRACK**   ☐ **DELETE**

TITLE:_____ NAME: _____ POSITION: _____

FIRM/COMPANY: _____

ADDRESS: _____SUITE: _____

CITY/STATE/ZIP: _____

INDUSTRY: _____ SOURCE (NAME): _____

BUSINESS PHONE: (_____) _____-_____

FAX #:   (_____) _____-_____   DATA ENTRY

HOME PHONE: (_____) _____-_____   BY:_____

CELL PHONE: (_____) _____-_____   DATE: _____/_____/_____

E-MAIL ADDRESS: _____

going to delegate the input of data, an easy way of managing the project is to simply staple a business card of the person you want to add to the form. Then, request that your assistant initial and return the form to you once the information has been added.

Cast a wide net

In deciding who to add to your contact list, we recommend that you add as many names as possible. Selling is a numbers game and you never know for sure where business could come from. Our clients are often surprised that business gets referred from unlikely sources. So, as a rule, you should cast a wide net. Apply the two standards for quality targets: The potential of leading to business, and likeability. In time, you may review your list and make deletions. But once names are deleted, they may be forgotten forever.

Tracking

As you learn that people move, make sure that you track them and update their information. One common way of getting business is when your contacts move from one company to another. But it is easy to lose track of people. So, when you learn that someone has moved or changed employment, develop the habit of getting their new contact information.

One of our clients told the story of how she built her business by staying in touch with many of her contacts. She did business with banks, and during an economic down-turn, many of her contacts lost their jobs. During that period she was diligent in tracking them. And, when they finally relocated with new banks, she found that she was able to keep her relationships with their prior employers and form new ones as well.

> ▼
> ✍ Comfort zone task—Find a contact database and start inputting your contact data.

Once you have the foundation of a mailing list, you are in a position to do many things. You can send newsletters and reprints of articles to your contacts. You can notify them of seminars and other activities you are doing. And, you can go through your list to identify the names of specific targets that you want to prioritize.

Individual Outreach

With a mailing list or contact database system in place, the next issue is individual outreach. Some of your contacts are going to stand out as having greater promise, and it may be worth giving these contacts individual attention. For this, we have created the Relationship Development Worksheet, shown in Exhibit C.

Exhibit C—Relationship Development Worksheet

☐ **Added to Contact Data Base**
☐ **Visited Web Site**

RELATIONSHIP DEVELOPMENT WORKSHEET

Contact Name: _____   **Phone:** _____

Qualifications: _____

Company: _____   **Source:** _____ ☐ **Thanked**

Secretary/Assistant: _____   **Email:** _____

☐ **Team Target**   **Team Members:** _____

Spouse/Significant Other: _____

Children: _____

Mutual Contacts: _____   *Potential Introductions:* _____

Organizations: _____   *Publications* _____

Hobbies/Interests: _____   *Needs:* _____

Market Research: _____

THE SELLING PROCESS: ☐ **Meet** ☐ **Build Trust** ☐ **Clarify Needs** ☐ **Get Approved** ☐ **Close**

POTENTIAL VALUE-IN-ADVANCE: Educate; Entertain; Introduce; Inspire; Provide Leadership

Date	Notes	Action	"Do" Date

Reproduced with permission of Kohn Communications (**www.kohncommunications.com**).

As we mentioned earlier in this book, building relationships is a process that involves building trust, clarifying needs, getting approved and ultimately closing. The relationship development worksheet is designed to facilitate this process. The worksheet will help you to accumulate and document information about your contacts that will help you strengthen each relationship. It will help you determine what stage you are at in the selling process and what steps need to be taken to achieve your goals. And, it will ensure that none of your valuable contacts slip through the cracks.

The benefit of having a checklist

The worksheet serves as a checklist. If you look at the worksheet, you can see several issues that it prompts you to think about, and tasks that it reminds you to do. Using this form as a checklist will help you speed up the relationship-building process, and make it more comfortable.

Having a checklist allows you to be more thorough and organized in any endeavor. Before you fly an airplane, do you rely on memory or do you review a checklist? When NASA launches a space shuttle, does someone say, "Well, did we check everything?" Or, do they go through an extensive checklist?

Of course, selling is not rocket science. Nevertheless, there is too much information to remember, especially if you are dealing with hundreds of contacts over a period of many years.

> ▼
> Having a checklist speeds up the relationship-building process.

Basic tasks

In the upper right-hand corner, there are two check boxes. One check box reminds you to add each contact to your contact database, or mailing list. This is important because if you get busy and are unable to follow-up personally with a particular target, at least you can stay in touch when you communicate to the entire list.

The second check box reminds you to visit the contact's Web site. Often, a target's Web site will help you learn more about the person's business and give ideas for things to comfortably talk about.

Contact information

Next, write down the contact's name, phone, email address and company. It is valuable to have this contact information at your fingertips so that you don't have to look it up. It may seem like a small point but actually, one of the reasons people don't follow up with their contacts is that they can't remember where they placed a phone number or email address. And, while they are looking for it they get distracted by something else and forget about making the call.

Qualifications

On the qualifications line, write down your reasons for pursuing each contact. For example, if someone is a prospect, write down your reasons why. Is this person a decision maker? Does this company need your services? If the contact is a referral source, does he have good contacts? Knowing that you are pursuing qualified targets will increase your enthusiasm for selling.

Source

We always recommend putting the source on the worksheet so that you remember how you met someone. After meeting lots of people, it becomes more difficult to remember everyone. You may see a name on your worksheet but not remember that person. Remembering the referral source or the place where you met someone helps to remind you who each person is. Also, if you consistently document your sources of business, you may notice trends that will be helpful in your future selling.

If you met via a referral source, the worksheet reminds you to thank that person. It is difficult to develop quality referral sources, so it is always important to show your appreciation when referral sources think of you.

Secretary/Assistant

We also have a place on the worksheet for the name of the Secretary/Assistant. Secretaries, assistants, and even receptionists are *gatekeepers*. A lot of people consider gatekeepers to be barriers. However, we see the gatekeepers as potential allies. They can help you track down your contacts, let you know the best times to call, and make sure that your messages get priority treatment.

An important tip for turning the gatekeepers into allies is to remember their names. When they answer the phone, you can use their names. That will signal to them that you have had interaction with them in the past. That will make them feel more comfortable and willing to be of assistance. So, remember to write down their names.

Team target

This category is designed to remind you to consider whether or not there are other people in your firm or company that share this target and to help you decide whether you want to pursue the target with a team or independently. If you want to pursue the target as a team, check the box and list the names of the team members who you think should be included in the selling effort.

Significant data

In the shaded area, the worksheet asks you to document information about your contacts that will help you identify opportunities for building each relationship and to feel more emotionally connected to your contacts. As we discuss the following categories of information, keep in mind that just because you write something down doesn't mean that you are obligated to use it. Rather, you want to remember important details so that you have the option to raise these issues if you feel it is appropriate. But, if you don't record significant data, then you may miss valuable relationship-building opportunities.

Spouse/Significant other

There may be circumstances when it is beneficial to know the names of your contacts' spouses or significant others. Remembering this information can help strengthen emotional bonds with your targets. Occasionally, you may be interested in inquiring about them. Or, if you call your contacts to invite them to a family-oriented activity, such as dinner or a party, you will feel more comfortable if you can remember the names of their spouses or significant others.

Children

Similarly, remembering children's names is a way of feeling more emotionally connected with your targets. If you have children, remembering that your contacts have children of similar age may stimulate ideas of things you can do together.

One of our clients worked at a firm that provided tickets to different types of events. Being a junior partner, our client got tickets to the circus instead of the basketball games, and he felt dejected. We pointed out that many of his contacts have children, and that he should use those tickets to entertain his targets' families. Seizing on our idea, he invited a prospect and his children to the circus. At the event, his contact put his arm around our client's shoulder and said, "This has been such a great experience. My kids are really enjoying the circus. And, I have gotten an opportunity to get to know you, and I want to do business with you." In reporting this story to us, our client was so happy about his success that he nearly cried.

Mutual contacts

Remembering if you have mutual contacts is another way of feeling emotionally connected. It reminds you that you are a part of this person's community. Think of a time when you met a stranger at some event, and then learned that you both had a mutual friend. This awareness can immediately increase your mutual feeling of safety and connectedness.

Potential introductions

The worksheet asks you to think about potential introductions that your targets could make. If your targets work in companies, maybe they could introduce you to their colleagues. Your targets may have friends in other businesses that may be prospects for you. Maybe your targets have advisors they could introduce you to. For example, if you get work from CPAs, ask yourself, "Have you met the CPAs of all of your clients?"

Organizations
The worksheet asks you to consider what organizations your targets belong to. Some of your targets may belong to organizations in which you could meet and get to know other promising targets.

Publications
The worksheet asks you to consider what publications your targets read. Reading these publications may give you greater insight into the trends and needs of your targets' industries. It may give you things to talk about with your contacts. Also, these publications may provide writing or advertising opportunities for you.

Hobbies and interests
Knowing your contacts' hobbies and interests may give you ideas for things you can do together to strengthen your relationships. We have had many clients build their books of business based on shared interests and hobbies. Shared passions such as music, cooking, or sports, often provide things to talk about and reasons for getting together.

Needs
The worksheet asks you to think about potential needs that your target may have. If you can think of some value to offer to your contact, then that might be an appropriate reason to call.

Market research
Use this section to document any market research you do. If you have a prospect, you may want to check out their Web site or do Internet searches to find information that may give you a competitive advantage.

The selling process check-boxes
In the lower half of the form, we help you identify the steps for building relationships. The selling process check boxes remind you that selling is a process, and that there are stages in each relationship. Perhaps you have met someone, built trust, and clarified needs, and now it is time to get approved. Keep in mind that although we have displayed these stages in a linear fashion, this is not necessarily a step-by-step process. You may have been approved but are still not getting work and so you may need to go back to clarify needs or build more trust.

List of potential "value-in-advance"

The list of value-in-advance reminds you of the types of value that you can offer to build relationships. Perhaps you can offer to do a seminar or take someone to lunch. You may want to go back to Chapter 6 and review the various methods of giving value-in-advance.

Notes

Notes refer to the action you have taken. When you leave a message for someone, write down the date and the fact that you have a left a message. After you completed a task, such as having lunch, write it down so that you remember.

The importance of notes

People are constantly telling us that they don't have to take notes because they will remember what they have done. The fact is that you can't remember everything.

When you have something fresh in your mind it doesn't seem possible to forget and yet, you do. It is one of the reasons people don't follow up. They forget what they talked about with a target.

We had a client who didn't feel comfortable calling a contact until he remembered that during their last meeting, his target had suggested that they get together for lunch. Remembering this fact made our client feel at ease about calling and saying, "Last time we spoke, you suggested that we have lunch and now I am calling to schedule that lunch."

If you always remember to keep notes, then even after several years it will be easy to pick up the thread of a relationship. So, get in the habit of writing down notes about every conversation with your targets.

Action

Action refers to your next step. It is always a good idea to think about the next step in each relationship you are trying to develop.

In some cases, the next step may be obvious. You may know, for example, that it is time to take someone to lunch. In some cases, however, the next step may not be obvious. If, for some reason, you are unable to think of next step, having the worksheet gives you the ability to go back to it later. If nothing else, your action could be to review this contact again after a period of time, or discuss this contact with one of your colleagues. We have found that reviewing your follow-up strategies with people whose opinions you respect usually results in coming up with ideas for action-items.

We have so many examples of this in our coaching. We have had clients who were adamant that they couldn't think of a way to follow up with a particular contact. But after a little brainstorming, they were able to think of comfortable and sensible follow-up strategies. Review Chapters 6 and 7 for some ideas for action-items to schedule.

Due date

Finally, once you have decided on an action, we recommend writing down a specific date for when you plan to take action. Then, put the person's name in your calendar on that day so that you don't forget.

A lot of people are not in the habit of scheduling tasks. Maybe they keep a to-do list instead. The problem with to-do lists is that it is based on the theory that you will implement your tasks when you have time. Most people that we know have very little time and so they don't complete their tasks. When you put something in your calendar, you pick a time that is practical for implementing the task. People tend to respect their calendars. When something is in your calendar, it is more likely to get done.

Create a worksheet for every target

We recommend that you keep a relationship development worksheet for each primary contact that we helped you identify in Chapter 5. Every time you take some action, get in the habit of updating the respective worksheets.

We also recommend keeping your worksheets in a three-ring binder on your desk or somewhere in plain sight so that when it is time to contact someone, or when one of your contacts calls you, your notes are easily accessible. Keeping the binder in plain sight will also serve as a reminder that you need to be thinking about selling.

At first, using a new system to manage your relationships may seem like a burden and overly time consuming. But, in fact, just the reverse is true. The worksheets will make your selling effort easier.

The worksheets will help you save time. It is difficult to remember all of the information you have collected about your targets. Once you complete your worksheets, all of the information about all of your targets is available for a quick review.

Our clients regularly tell us that the worksheets keep them organized and focused on marketing. They acknowledge that the process of filling out the forms has resulted in doing more outreach and thinking of ideas for reaching out to contacts they would otherwise not have thought of. When we speak at conferences and retreats, we constantly run into past clients who say that they still keep their relationship development worksheet binders on their desks and use them regularly.

Hand-written versus computer

The system we have shown is a manual system. Although there are computer database programs that will do many of the same things, we recommend that you begin and learn the system manually. The problem with start-ing with a computer program is that in addition to developing the skill and habit of relationship development, you have to research, purchase, and learn how to use the software. This often creates a barrier to getting started.

Later, as you learn the skill and develop a sufficient number of con-tacts, you may want to convert to computer-based contact management software. There are many contact management computer programs avail-able, some for a few hundred dollars and some that cost several thousands of dollars.

Conclusion

An important part of the selling process is maintaining a positive and con-sistent presence in the lives of your targets. If you want to be successful in selling, it is imperative that you develop safe and effective systems for stay-ing in touch.

Skill Modules— Tips for Safe and Effective Selling Strategies

Tips for Public Speaking: How to Overcome Your Fear of Embarrassment and Maximize Your Success

ONE OF THE MOST EFFECTIVE SALES TOOLS is public speaking. Well-targeted public speaking can provide exposure to large numbers of quality prospects and referral sources, and position you as an authority in your field. Also, if your speech provides value to your audience, public speaking will not carry the stigma of selling.

However, a lot of people are uncomfortable with public speaking. They are afraid of being embarrassed in front of an audience. And, they are afraid of wasting time because of the time required to prepare, and because the audience may not be well targeted. To help you overcome these obstacles, we have provided some tips to help you make your public speaking both safe and effective.

> While you may not fear speaking more than death, that doesn't mean you're dying to do it.

We begin with tips for increasing your feelings of safety.

Overcome Your Fear of Public Speaking

Some people say they fear public speaking more than they fear death. While you may not fear speaking more than death, that doesn't mean you're dying to do it. The fact is, most people are

117

remarkably afraid to do public speaking. If you're afraid of it, you'll avoid it. And, avoiding it can limit your success. The anticipation of public speaking can be so physically, emotionally, and mentally debilitating that it reduces both productivity and quality of life for the entire time between the planning and the presentation.

Fear of speaking comes from the anticipation of being embarrassed. It's unnerving to imagine being judged in an unfavorable way. Usually, the reason people worry about being embarrassed is they have all kinds of misconceptions of what their audiences expect from them. They think their audiences want them to be smarter, or more articulate, or attractive, or funny, or charismatic, or dynamic, or inspirational, or motivational. They think their audiences expect them to memorize the material or know all the answers. All of these feelings of inadequacy will surely instill the fear of being embarrassed.

While a certain amount of stage fright is normal, you don't want your fear to be crippling. So, in order to help you reduce your fear, here are some practical tips. We focus on two components of your speech: content and delivery.

Tips for Crafting Quality Content

One of the most important techniques for overcoming your fear of embarrassment is to provide information that you genuinely believe will be of value to your audience. Audiences are primarily interested in receiving information they can use in their business and personal lives. If you have confidence that your content will be appreciated by your audience, you are less likely to fear embarrassment.

> ▼
> Confidence in your content will reduce your fear of embarrassment

Unfortunately, many professionals do not think of themselves as good writers. However, you don't have to be another Herman Melville or Ernest Hemingway. You just have to provide clear and useful information. Here are some tips on crafting quality speeches.

Tip 1: Pick a Topic That Is Important to You

One of the most important tips for writing a good speech is to pick a topic that is important to you. If possible, find something that you are passionate about. The more you care about your subject, the more time and effort you will be willing to invest in preparing your speech. A topic that is personally important to you will be more enjoyable to write, and engrossing to your audience.

Even if your topic is a dry, technical subject, you can find something about it that is interesting if you can make a personal, emotional connection. For example, we consulted to a pension actuary who did a lot of speaking to other actuaries on legislation impacting pension plans. It is hard to imagine a drier topic. But, he made his speeches interesting by discussing the impact these regulations had on the lives of the people who were covered by the retirement plan—their ability to retire with sufficient income and the risks of losing their benefits.

Tip 2: Pick a Subject That Is Important to Your Audience

The more confident you are that your topic is important to your audience, the more comfortable you will feel. If possible, talk to members of your audience well in advance of your speech. If you can't do that, talk with people who know your audience. Find out what they are interested in. Discuss their needs. Share some of your ideas and confirm if they are perceived as valuable. In this way, you can develop confidence that your topic will be valued.

Tip 3: Give Yourself Sufficient Time

A lot of people who are asked to speak on a topic that they know well are lulled into a false sense of security. They think because they know the topic, it will be easy to write about it. But, there is a huge difference between knowing a subject and writing about it. You may understand a topic and even be able to discuss it in conversation. But, when it comes time to putting ink to paper, it can be remarkably challenging to zero-in on the main issues and talk about them in a way that is clear, concise, organized, and useful.

So, whenever possible, give yourself plenty of lead time to write your speech. Good speeches often require brooding over the issues. The more time you invest in thinking and writing, the more excited you will be about delivering your speech, which will translate into greater confidence and quality.

Tip 4: Identify Your Main Message

The biggest challenge in writing a quality speech is becoming clear about what you want to say. Ask yourself, "What are the most important and useful points that you want your audience to know?" Once you answer this central question, the writing should become much easier. Everything you say in your speech should focus on helping people with those issues.

Tip 5: Write an Opening That Captures Attention

One of the ways you develop comfort in speaking is the belief that you can quickly capture audience attention. There are many approaches to writing an attention-grabbing opening.

State your objectives

Audiences want to quickly understand how you plan to help them. One of the best ways to open is to simply state your goals and objectives. In this way, the audience will know how they will benefit from your speech and that they should pay attention.

If we were writing a speech on the subject of this book, we might open by saying, "We are here today to talk about methods of selling in your comfort zone. Our goal is to help you change the way you think about selling." If you can clearly explain to the audience why your topic will help them, they'll pay attention.

The dilemma of telling jokes

You may have heard many speakers open with a joke or story. Jokes can be a good way to break the ice. But, they can also be very risky. Jokes are often insulting or not funny. Unless you are extremely skilled in telling jokes, we advise against it.

Tell a story

Another method for opening a speech is to tell a story which has the same main point as your speech. A story makes the point more interesting and memorable. It creates drama, and gives the speech direction. The story could be the history of your topic, or why you became interested. We recommend that you make your story personal. Personal stories are easy to tell and often relate well to an audience.

Tip 6: Explain Why Your Main Message Is Important

People want to know how your message will realistically help them succeed either in their work or in their personal lives. Stating why your message is important will help bolster your comfort and make your speech more interesting to your listeners.

Tip 7: Give Lots of Good Tips

Once you gain your audience's attention, you want to keep it for the duration of the program. An effective technique is to give lots of useful tips.

Good business speeches are characterized by good tips. You will feel more confident in speaking when you genuinely believe that you are providing useful information. We have had many clients who have said that if they can get one or two good tips from a speech, it would be worth their time. So, our philosophy is to give dozens of good tips. The more tips you fill your speech with, the more confident you will feel that it will be well-received.

> Good speeches are characterized by lots of tips.

Tip 8: Give Relevant Examples

Whenever possible, provide examples that clarify your main points. Preferably, use examples from your personal life or the lives of people you know. Examples give your speeches energy. They make your speeches more enjoyable to give and to listen to. They reveal more about your experience. And, knowing that you have interesting examples to share, will give you a greater feeling of confidence when you speak.

Tips for Improving Your Delivery

With a quality speech in hand, the next issue to be concerned with is your delivery. There are a few fundamental guidelines to follow that will help you deliver with confidence.

Tip 1: Breathe and Smile

It is a well-known fact that breathing and smiling help you relax. Each time you practice your speech, and when you actually deliver your speech, remember to take a couple of deep breaths, and smile. You may even want to put a reminder to breathe and smile in large print on your notes.

Tip 2: Decide Whether or Not to Use Notes

One of the great fears of public speaking is the fear that you may forget what to say. One common solution is to use notes.

There are many different opinions on whether or not to use notes. The answer depends on the nature of your speech and your circumstances.

The arguments against using notes

There are risks of using notes. You may refer to them too frequently and lose contact with the audience. Or, you may lose your place, which can be a disaster for your speech. Furthermore, if you are not dependent upon notes, it will be easier to be animated and maintain eye contact with the audience.

The arguments in favor of using notes

We believe it is absolutely appropriate to use notes if they help calm your nerves about remembering your speech. Your audience is probably more concerned with getting useful information than they are about whether or not you are using notes.

Tips for using notes

If you plan to use notes, you can learn how to use them in a way that appears natural and allows you to connect with your audience. Here are some tips for using notes effectively:

Print your notes on 8 x 11-1/2 sheets of paper instead of note cards so that they are easy to hold and read. If you put them down when you delve into a topic, large sheets are easier to find.

- Use a large font size, such as 20-points or more. A large font will help you see your notes, and still maintain contact with the audience.
- Use colored markers to identify important points.
- Use handouts and/or audio visuals. If you hand out an outline, you can refer to it to help both you and your audience stay on track. We often use a fill-in outline. A fill-in outline is a document that has head lines of main points but leaves out key information that you want you audience to fill in. This type of outline keeps the audience engaged.
- Audio-visuals, such as PowerPoint, also help you to stay on track. As you flip from one slide to the next, you are reminded of all of the points you want to make. Furthermore, well-designed audio-visuals can make your presentation more interesting. Just make sure that you don't use the audio-visual aid as text which you recite word for word. This can be boring for your audience. Never forget that you should be the center of attention, not your audio-visuals.

Tip 3: Memorize Your Open

Even is you plan to use notes, at minimum, we recommend memorizing your open. A lot of anxiety in speeches comes from the fear of not knowing what you are going to say when you are first introduced. Even if you know your material, there is often a surge of anxiety that is experienced just before you begin. If you have memorized and rehearsed your open, when you first look out into the sea of faces staring at you, the words are more likely comfortably slide off your lips. Most people report that once you get past the open, the whole speech becomes easier.

Reduce anxiety by memorizing your open.

Tip 4: Write Transitions

A lot of anxiety comes from not knowing how to transition from one point to the next. In your speech, make sure you write good transitions that help you close one section and introduce the next. It may be as simple as, "This concludes the current section. Let's move onto the next topic." Good transitions will allow you to comfortable move from issue to the next without stumbling.

Tip 5: Rehearse Your Speech

Practice delivering your speech aloud. Practice alone, practice with friends, record, and evaluate yourself. The more you practice and get feedback, the more you will improve your content and delivery, and the more confident you will be at the time of your speech.

Tip 6: Time Your Speech

A lot of anxiety results from not timing your presentation. If it isn't timed, you may find yourself three-quarters of the way through your time slot without covering a majority of your material. This causes you to rush and leave out information you planned on using.

As you write your speech, make sure you identify specific time slots for your main points. We recommend actually annotating your notes with time markers. You don't want to make the mistake of focusing too long on one point at the expense of the rest of the presentation. The issue of staying on time becomes more challenging when you encourage audience participation. Make sure that you don't stray too far from the main point and remember to check the time frequently. Consider putting a small clock on the lectern.

Tip 7: Ask for Evaluations

Speaker evaluations help you improve the quality of your speaking. Some organizations provide their own speaker evaluations for the audience to complete and return. If they do, ask to see them. If they don't have evaluations then bring your own. See Exhibit D for a sample speaker evaluation.

Tip 8: Do a Lot of Speaking

The more public speaking you do, the more comfortable you will become. We recommend finding environments to practice your public speaking. Begin by speaking in front of audiences that are supportive. For example, join a Toastmasters Club, or take a class in public speaking.

Maximize the Value of Public Speaking

As you become more comfortable with the process of public speaking, the next obstacle to overcome is to make your speeches a good use of your time. To maximize the value of your speeches, you want get exposure to quality targets, bond with your audience, and reveal positive qualities about yourself. Here are some tips to increase your success.

Tip 1: Find Quality Targets

Unless the purpose of your speech is simply to practice and you don't care about generation business, then you need to make sure that your audiences are selected wisely. Refer to the chapter on targeting.

Exhibit D—Program Evaluation Form

Instructor: _____

Program: _____

Location: _____

Your Name: _____ Date: _____

Please circle the number that reflects your opinion. (1=poor, 10=excellent)

1. Overall value of the program: 1 2 3 4 5 6 7 8 9 10

Comments: _____
_____
_____

2. Teaching skills of the instructor: 1 2 3 4 5 6 7 8 9 10

Comments: _____
_____
_____

3. Likelihood of implementing what you ve learned: 1 2 3 4 5 6 7 8 9 10

Comments: _____
_____
_____

4. What did you find most valuable? _____
_____
_____

5. What would you have excluded? _____
_____
_____

6. What wasn t included that you would like to learn? _____
_____
_____

Tip 2: Meet People as They Arrive

If possible, meet members of the audience as they arrive. Instead of standing at the lectern while waiting for the audience to sit down, stand at the entrance and greet people as they enter. Introduce yourself as the speaker. Ask them if there are any particular issues they have come to learn. This may help you personalize your speech and make it more valuable to your audience. Also, when you personally connect with your audience, they will be more attentive during your speech, more likely to participate, and more likely to come up to you afterwards.

Tip 3: Write Your Own Introduction

Ideally, the host should prepare the audience so that they will be optimistic and enthusiastic about your presentation. However, very few people are trained in the art of Master of Ceremonies. So, you should always write your own introduction for the host to read. Describe the reasons why you are qualified to speak on the topic and how you provide value.

If the host knows you personally, you might ask him or her to personalize the introduction with a statement such as, "I am pleased to introduce someone who I have known for many years and who is highly knowledgeable in this topic."

Tip 4: Encourage Audience Participation

Another way to improve your speech is to promote audience participation. Try to ask questions and stimulate discussion. As you stimulate the audience to think, you will maintain their interest. To maximize the effectiveness of this approach, be sure that you are supportive of their remarks. Be careful not to criticize or embarrass anyone. Even subtle negativity will discourage continued participation.

If you plan on asking questions to stimulate audience participation, make sure that you ask questions which the audience will be motivated to answer. A common mistake speakers make is asking questions which require a specific answer. It is a technique many of us learned from our teachers and professors. However, instead of stimulating a response, this approach will actually inhibit audience participation. Members of the audience will feel embarrassed for either not knowing the answer, or worse, giving the wrong answer. A superior approach is to ask the audience about their attitudes and experiences concerning the issues being discussed. Ask them what problems they have encountered and how they have solved those problems. If given the opportunity, audiences will be enthusiastic about sharing their feelings and opinions. And, at the same time, you will gain greater insight into their needs.

Tip 5: Maintain Eye Contact

Eye contact is an effective technique for creating an emotional bond. Rather than looking out to the general audience, try to look directly in the eyes of every attendee. The best approach is to think of your speech as a conversation with individuals. So, as you speak, keep talking to someone directly. You can actually maintain eye contact for a longer period of time than you may imagine. Instead of darting your eyes around the room, you can focus on one person for up to 10 or 15 seconds. If it is a large room, try to make eye contact with as many people as possible.

Tip 6: Avoid Frowning

An effective tool for bonding with the audience is a slight smile, even while you are talking. It sends a message that you are a nice person who is happy to be speaking and happy with your audience. Too often, people appear too serious and that can be misinterpreted as unhappy or uncomfortable. Those emotions push people away.

On the other hand, you don't want to maintain a Cheshire cat grin. The best smile is a Mona Lisa smile. Of course, there may be moments when scowling or frowning benefits the speech. But, most the time, remember, "Smile and the world smiles with you."

Tip 7: Create Opportunities for Follow-through

Throughout the speech, one of your goals is to create mechanisms for furthering the relationship with your targets in the audience. The standard approach is to give your information and hope that someone will be motivated to hire you. However, people may forget about you. You should look for ways to maintain consistent and positive presence with your targets. See Chapter 9 on staying in touch.

> Maximize the value of speaking by creating opportunities to follow up with attendees.

Tip 8: Create a Call to Action

One of the ways you open the door to future interaction with your prospects is to make a call to action. At the end of your speech, you can offer some activity in which you invite them to participate. For example, you could invite them to join organizations in which you are involved. You could enlist their assistance on some project you may be implementing. Or, you could suggest that they participate in round-tables or brainstorming sessions you are coordinating. The more valuable the offer, the more likely you will find eager participants which will enhance the likelihood of developing an alliance and ultimately acquiring a client.

Tip 9: Request a Business Card

Another effective technique for furthering interaction is to motivate members of the audience to give you their business cards. During your speech, offer to add interested prospects to your mailing list by promising to send them newsletters, articles, surveys, reports, or other informative correspondence. Offer to send them invitations to programs such as seminars or workshops. Experience has demonstrated that after a speech, when members of the audience return to their offices, the pressures of their lives take over. Even if they intend to call you, they are likely to procrastinate or forget. A successful marketing speech always provides many reasons for prospects to give you their cards.

▼
Increase the likelihood of ongoing interaction by getting the card.

Conclusion

Speaking is a valuable method for meeting quality prospects and referral sources, and positioning yourself as an authority. Don't allow your fear of embarrassment or your concern that it wastes time to stop you. As we have demonstrated, there are many sensible techniques for overcoming your fear of public speaking and maximizing its benefits.

Tips for Conducting Effective Seminars

SEMINARS ARE AN EFFECTIVE TECHNIQUE for meeting new people and cementing relationships with existing contacts. They build credibility, showcase the expertise of the members of your firm, and provide valuable networking opportunities for clients, prospects, and referral sources.

Seminars are a proven technique for getting additional work from existing clients and referral sources, as well as inspiring prospects to hire you. They provide a comfortable reason for communicating with your targets. In fact, even if people don't attend your seminars, there is still value in making the invitation.

One of our clients received a small response when he conducted a seminar. Only three people sent RSVPs. Closer to the event, two of them had to cancel due to schedule conflicts, and so our client cancelled the seminar. But under our direction, he subsequently met with all three prospects at their offices and got business from two of them.

With seminars, you don't have to wait to be invited to speak for a group. Rather, you can plan them for any time or location. You can invite people to attend seminars in your office. You can rent a facility such as a hotel or restaurant. Or, you can take them to your targets' places of business.

The Reasons for Reluctance to Conduct Seminars

A lot of professionals are reluctant to conduct seminars. There are many reasons for this reluctance.

The Belief That Seminars Have to Be Large, Costly Events

When you think of seminars, it is easy to imagine large and costly events that attract hundreds of people. While large events are certainly exciting, seminars don't have to be large to be successful. We have conducted many seminars in which we invited a few good clients, prospects, or referrals to come to small get-togethers after work to have cocktails and engage in a discussion.

If you don't have much experience conducting seminars, we recommend beginning with small events. It may be worthwhile to invite just a select handful of high-quality targets. Small seminars are low cost and easy to orchestrate. And, the intimate setting of small events facilitates quality interaction. After developing practice in conducting small seminars, you can graduate to larger events.

> Start small. Small seminars are easier, less costly and create a more intimate environment.

Small seminars can be done inexpensively if you have a board room. Or, you can do them at a hotel or restaurant.

A very effective and inexpensive technique is to hold them on-site at your targets' businesses. By going out to the locations of your prospects, clients, and referral sources, you can cement your relationships with your contact and meet the other people at those businesses.

The obstacle of picking a topic

Professionals are reluctant to conduct seminars because they lack confidence in choosing a hot topic. The solution here is to realize that hot new topics are not a requirement for a successful seminar. Just about any issue you are helping a client on is a potential subject. It is logical to assume that if one client is having a problem, there are prospects out there that are experiencing it, too.

The concern over competition

Another reason for reluctance to do seminars is the perception that too many of your competitors are already conducting seminars. This is self-defeating thinking. Even if your competitors are actively giving seminars, it is unlikely that quality targets have had their fill of quality speakers and programs.

If your competitors are doing seminars, it is because there is a good reason. And, by refraining from doing seminars, you are allowing them to own that territory.

Tips for Successful Seminars

Once you've decided to conduct a seminar, you want it to run smoothly. Here are twelve tips to maximize your success.

Tip 1: Anticipate a Modest Response Rate

Response rates will vary based on the recognition of your firm's name, the topic's significance, the perception of need, the distance that targets must travel, and the cost of attendance. It also depends on whether you invite strangers or people you know. If you invite strangers, you can anticipate a lower turn out. Even if you receive a lot of RSVPs, you can anticipate a high percentage of no-shows among strangers. So, it makes sense to anticipate a modest response rate. If you underestimate the response rate, your worst problem would be a huge turn out. If your venue is too small to accommodate a larger turn out, then you can conduct the same seminar several times.

Tip 2: Clean up Your Invitation List before Mailing

If you buy a list, it may be full of errors. Call invitees to confirm the accuracy of their addresses. Ask if this is the right person to invite and, if not, find out who is.

If you are mailing to your own contacts, use the seminar as a reason to update addresses and phone numbers. This will help you for future outreach.

Tip 3: Make Phone Calls

It is a good idea to call people in advance to tell them to expect an invitation and to hold the date in their calendars. Once the invitations are out, phone as many of the invitees as possible and recommend that they attend. Tell them to put it in their calendars. If they can't attend, suggest that they send an alternate. Finally, before the event, call again to remind them to attend. This three-call rule will ensure the largest possible attendance.

> ▼
> Use the 3-call rule to ensure the largest turnout.

Tip 4: Consider Joint Venture Partners

If you implement a seminar with other non-competing businesses, each can invite their targets and share the cost of the event.

Tip 5: Include a Guest Speaker Who Is a Draw

Many well-known people with their own outreach agendas will speak for free or a modest fee. Even a high fee could be justified if the presence of a celebrity will attract your targets.

Tip 6: Send Invitations by Email

This technique's success has been astounding. People often respond more to email than to regular mail. In some cases, we've seen response rates of up to 98 percent, meaning that 98 percent communicated either a "yes" or a "no."

Tip 7: Provide Several Ways to RSVP

Give your phone and fax numbers, email address, and a mail-back response form along with your invitation.

Tip 8: Make All Attendees Feel Welcome

Make it easy to find parking and your venue. Have employees and partners greet all attendees at the door. Provide name tags. Have a friendly staff person for registration. If someone isn't on the attendance list, don't appear concerned. Simply smile, give them a name tag and usher them in. If you know the attendees, introduce them to each other. And, definitely validate parking.

Tip 9: Make the Seminar Interesting

Make sure all content is clear, concise, and valuable to the audience. Include lots of tips and practical advice. And, keep the program moving. Provide a fast-paced, stimulating experience that leaves the audience wanting to come back for more. Refer to Skill Module 1, for tips on creating quality content in your speeches.

Tip 10: Bond with Your Audience

Use the tips in Skill Module 1 for bonding with your audience to establish rapport and credibility and increasing the likelihood that people will want to hire you. Also, refer to Chapter 7, which discusses direct and indirect methods for revealing your interest in doing business with your targets.

Tip 11: Follow Up

After the seminar, be sure to follow up with each attendee. Thank them for attending and get their feedback. Ask for future topic suggestions. Remember that follow-up is the key to your success in getting new business. Refer to Chapter 9 for follow-up techniques.

Tip 12: Experiment with the Elements of Your Seminars

If you continue to conduct seminars in the future, experiment with time periods to maximize your success. For example, some people prefer seminars in the morning, others prefer programs in the afternoon, some like Mondays, others like Fridays. Modify the seminars to produce the most attendance possible.

Conduct Webcasts

Another way to conduct seminars is to do them over the Internet. Technology allows you to conduct inexpensive seminars using your telephone and

Web site. Attendees can dial-in and listen to you as you speak, and watch a presentation on their computer screens. You can give them the option to participate by asking questions over the phone or via email. While Webcasts are not as effective a developing personal rapport, many of our clients use Webcasts effectively for communicating with large numbers of clients and prospects.

In addition to the above tips for successful seminars, here are a few tips specifically for Webcasts.

Tip 1: Make It a Comfortable Experience

A lot of people are unfamiliar with computers. Make sure you provide clear and accurate instructions for accessing the Webcast. And, make sure they can contact someone if they are experiencing problems.

Tip 2: Create Interesting Visuals

Since you can't know if your audience is listening, make sure that your visuals are interesting. Find attractive photographs that are related to what you are saying. Create images that move. Provide clear, concise bullet points.

Tip 3: Record and Post Your Webcasts

Webcasts are broadcast at a specific time. So, you may want to record your webcasts to make them available on your Web site. Then, people can view them at their leisure.

Conclusion

The only way to really develop your ability to implement a successful seminar is to go ahead and conduct one. Don't try for a big event. Start small, but make it happen. In time, you may find that seminars are a highly effective technique for meeting new people and building quality relationships.

Tips for Effective and Affordable Public Relations

PUBLIC RELATIONS CAN BE a highly useful tool in your sales effort. While there are many forms of public relations, the most effective types are:

1. Public speaking
2. Publishing articles
3. Getting quoted
4. Producing events

These activities are effective in helping you develop business because they help you gain exposure to new targets and maintain a consistent and positive presence in the minds of your existing contacts.

A lot of people are reluctant to try public relations because they believe that it requires hiring expensive public relations firms. Since your efforts can take a long time to bare fruit, public relations can seem like a black hole into in which you pour money without any apparent results. But actually, you can learn how to do many aspects of public relations yourself effectively and affordably.

Here are some tips for effectively and affordably implementing your own public relations.

Acquire Public Speaking Opportunities

Getting public speaking engagements can be a relatively easy, inexpensive, and highly effective public relations technique.

Many organizations produce events and need speakers. Any one who has worked on an event planning committee knows how difficult the job of finding quality speakers can be. By reaching out and introducing yourself as a speaker to the right organizations, you may find that well-targeted speaking opportunities are well within your reach.

Tips for Arranging Speeches

Here are some tips for getting invited to speak.

Tip 1: Target the Right Organizations

Unless you are speaking for practice, you want get in front of quality targets. So, the first step in implementing a public speaking campaign is to identify the organizations that cater to your prospects and referral sources.

As we mentioned in Chapter 8, there are many types of organizations to consider. You should review that chapter now for ideas.

One type of organization that you should definitely consider is trade organizations that represent your existing clients' industries. You may also be able to find your targets in non-profit organizations, such as charities. Ask your clients, friends, and colleagues what organizations they are aware of.

There are also lists of professional organizations on the Internet or at the library. Search by industry or profession to find associations attended by your targets.

Tip 2: Identify the Contact Person

Once you have identified some organizations, the next step is to identify the right person to contact. There may be either a volunteer or staff-person in charge of finding speakers. Or, there may be a committee in charge of putting on events. Find out the name of the chairperson.

Tip 3: Identify Hot Topics

Identify topics that appeal to your target groups. One tip for selecting interesting topics is to consider the issues you are presently helping your clients with. Make a list of the questions your clients are asking you. The answers to these questions are often the basis of quality speeches.

Look for topics that are newsworthy or that have relevance to the audiences you are targeting. The more interesting the topics are to your targets, the more likely you'll be invited to speak.

Tip 4: Submit a Proposal

You may be asked to submit a proposal describing your topics and your experience. Your proposal should include a list of topics on which you are willing to speak. It should also include your bio and a list of any speeches you have already given. If you have published articles, then describe them as well.

Tip 5: Follow Up

Once someone has expressed interest and you have sent your media kit, make sure that you follow up. Don't be dissuaded simply because you haven't heard from the organization. People who book speakers on behalf of an organization are often volunteers or they are staff people who do many jobs. Even if they are interested in having you speak, they may forget to call you. Getting speaking engagements requires persistence. It is your job to follow up.

Tip 6: Delegate the Job of Finding Speaking Opportunities

The job of researching, making calls, and following up can be a time-consuming job. If you are too busy to do the job yourself, it can be delegated. Look for someone who is organized, friendly, professional, patient, and persistent.

There can be a lot of contacts to call, so it is helpful to use a spreadsheet to keep track of everyone who has been contacted, what was discussed, and when the follow-up is scheduled. You may want to use the Public Speaking Opportunity Report in Exhibit E. This can be easily set up in Microsoft Excel.

Get Published

Another effective way of supporting your selling effort is to write articles for publication. Articles do not have the same impact as public speaking. You cannot engage your audience with an article as you can with a speech. Furthermore, you are not present to meet your audience when they read your articles. You are relying on them to contact you.

But, there are still many benefits of getting published. Well-written articles can help you break through the barriers of skepticism. They provide tangible evidence that you are knowledgeable and have the ability to help people. If your articles are published, you gain third-party endorsement from the publisher that you are an authority in your field.

Articles are tangible. If people like your article, they may keep it for future reference. We've had experiences in which prospects have saved our articles for years, and then finally called us when they needed our services. Also, many of the articles we've had published have been re-published by other journals, providing even greater exposure.

Many of the tips for getting your articles published are the same as for getting speaking engagements.

Exhibit E—Public Relations Spreadsheet

Caller name: _____
Date: _____

CONTACT	TITLE	ASSOCIATION	DEMOGRAPHICS	CITY	PHONE	E-MAIL	PAST ACTION NEXT STEP

Tip 1: Find the Right Publications

You want to find publications that are read by your targets. While not all publications publish freelance articles, many are hungry for quality articles.

This reminds us of a story in which we submitted an article to a newspaper and after it was published, the editor asked: "Do you have any more articles? I've got a beast to feed. This is a daily newspaper and we always need good articles."

Tip 2: Find the Contact Person

As with speaking, you need to find the right person to contact. This is often the editor, whose name is typically identified in the publication. You can usually call this person directly. Just remember that it is always your job to follow up. Editors are busy, particularly as their publications approach deadline.

Tip 3: Identify Hot Topics

As with public speaking, you want to identify hot topics. Review the publications that clients and prospects read. Identify topics they are writing about, and topics they are missing. Even if there are other articles on your topic, you still may be able to write about it. Publications often have many articles on the same topic, but written from different angles. The main point is that you want an article that *you* have written that documents *your* expertise.

Tip 4: Submit an Outline or a Draft

You may be requested to submit an outline. However, it is often a better strategy to write the article first, and then submit it. If one publication doesn't use it, you can submit it to others.

Tip 5: Get Started

One of the biggest obstacles is writing the article, not finding someone to publish it. Writing is a daunting task that is easily postponed.

We recommend that you make a commitment to yourself and get started. Better yet, make a commitment to a publication. You will be more motivated to make the time if you have a deadline. Also, block time in your calendar that you can devote to writing. Consider making it short periods of time so that it doesn't seem overwhelming. Commit thirty minutes to write an introductory paragraph or an outline. Then, schedule more time to keep working on it. Once you get started, the momentum of writing will begin to take over and it will seem to become easier to find time.

Tip 6: Give Lots of Tips

As with your speaking, good business articles are characterized by lots of tips. Remember, your goal is to demonstrate your knowledge and to communicate that you offer value. Very few things communicate knowledge and value as well as an article with lots of good tips. People who read your articles and benefit from your advice are more likely to contact you when they need assistance.

We recommend an article-writing formula that we use and that you have seen illustrated all throughout this book. The formula is to identify a problem that your clients are having, explain the benefits of solving the problem, and then give tips for how to solve it.

Tip 7: Keep It Short

We recommend short, concise articles. These are easier to write, less time consuming, and publications often prefer short articles. Readers like short articles, which also can be used to fill space easily in a publication. For public relations purposes, you don't have to write a highly researched article. Write about something you know well that gives some good advice. All you need is a short article that paints a picture of credibility. Think of articles as "snapshots of credibility."

Tip 8: Use Lots of Bullet Points

You may have noticed that our writing style uses lots of bullet point and titles. These make your articles more readable. Use them frequently.

Tip 9: Use a Ghostwriter, If Necessary

If you are too busy to write it yourself, there are a lot of professional writers who can take your ideas and convert them into well-written articles. You can submit your thoughts in writing, or they can interview you and then draft an article for your review. Ghostwriters can provide a relatively inexpensive solution to getting the job done.

There is no shame in having a ghostwriter. Many well-known books are ghost-written. The article still contains your ideas. And, you have the final say in how it appears.

Tip 10: Post It on Your Web Site

Once published, add the article to your Web site. Then, you have the ability to send emails to your contacts with a link to your article. This is a highly effective technique for drawing traffic to your Web site and having people see that you are published. Even if you don't get an article published, you can still put it on your Web site.

Tip 11: Delegate the Placement

As with public speaking, you can delegate the job of placing articles. See Tip 6 for delegating the job of finding speaking opportunities.

Get Quoted or Mentioned in the Press

It is a great experience when someone from the press calls to quote you as an authority, or better yet, write an article about you or your firm. There are ways of increasing the likelihood of being identified for these opportunities.

Tip 1: Meet the Press

Get to know the writers and editors of the publications you are targeting. Think of these people as you would any target you want to build a relationship with. Meet them and explain how you are an authority in your field. Take them to lunch to get to know them better. Maintain a positive and consistent presence by sending articles that you write and announcements of speeches you give. And, then when they call to ask a question on some article they are writing, make sure that you are available.

Tip 2: Identify an Angle

Sometimes you can get publications to write articles about you or your firm if there is an angle that is considered newsworthy. Publications may be interested if there is something unusual about your firm's philosophy or history. If you are a lawyer and recently won a ground-breaking case, then legal publications might be interested. Issues that are controversial are also interesting. If you can't think of an angle, you may want to contact the editors and writers of the publications and ask them what they are looking for.

Tip 3: Send Announcements

At minimum, you can often get certain business publications to print announcements about news in your firm. You can send announcements if you recently won an award, closed a large deal, or someone joined your firm. Often, these announcements get published.

Produce Events

Another effective form of public relations can be inviting people to events such as parties, seminars, forums, and fund-raising events. Events have great value because they help you maintain a positive presence in the lives of your contacts. They can be entertaining, informative, and allow you to introduce your contacts to each other.

People are more likely to come to an event when they know that it will be fun and interesting, or that there will be other people in attendance who they want to meet. If you are conducting a seminar, then follow the rules for effective seminars discussed in Skill Module 2: Conducting Effective Seminars. If you are planning a party, here are two tips to make them more successful:

Tip 1: Pick an Interesting Venue

You have many options for where to hold events. You can do them at your office, at restaurants or hotels. Many of our clients have hosted parties at museums and historic buildings. You can even do them at home.

Tip 2: Select a Cause

You can make your events appealing by tying them to a non-profit cause. Many of our clients support local charities. If you are interested in politics, consider throwing a party in support of someone's campaign.

Hire a Publicist

If you decide that you simply don't want to do the public relations yourself, you can always hire a professional publicist to assist you with all or some aspects of your public relations campaign. If this is the case, then here are two important characteristics to look for.

1. Look for a publicist who is willing to work on an hourly or project basis rather than a long-term monthly retainer. In this way, you can experiment with public relations and determine whether or not it is right for you without committing to a long-term contract.

2. Look for a publicist who is willing to provide you with a progress report of the people contacted on your behalf and the follow-up that is scheduled. Some publicists consider this to be proprietary information and refuse to share it. However, we believe that having this information is critical to your success for three reasons. First, seeing a progress report will help you learn about the public relations process. Second, a progress report will help you monitor your publicist's activities. And third, if for any reason you lose you publicist, you won't lose the information necessary to continue your public relations effort.

Conclusion

Public relations can be an extremely effective method for meeting new people and building trust and rapport with existing contacts, whether you handle it yourself or outsource to professionals. Although it may take a long time to see results, it can become an extremely successful and integral part of your sales effort.

Tips for Documenting the Value That You Offer

AN IMPORTANT COMPONENT of feeling comfortable with selling is to have promotional documents that you are proud of and that help you build trust. There is probably no one document that is going to convince your prospects to hire you. Rather, your promotional documents are a part of the selling process. They paint a picture of you as someone who is trustworthy and offers value. Think of your documents as "snapshots of credibility."

There are several types of promotional documents that create snapshots of credibility, including:

- Brochures
- Fact sheets
- Biographies
- Testimonials
- Articles
- Newsletters
- The tools of your trade
- Credibility kits
- Web sites

Brochures

A brochure is probably the most commonly used promotional document. Prospects frequently ask to see them. And yet, ironically, they are often the least influential part of the selling process. Brochures frequently are not read or retained by prospects.

145

So, we typically don't recommend that you spend a lot of money on brochures. Rather, you should spend just enough to create a document of which you can feel proud.

One of the great benefits of creating a brochure is actually the writing process. By thinking and discussing the content of your brochure, you can gain greater clarity about the value that you offer to your clients. Here are some things you may want to include in your brochure:

1. Your philosophy for doing business. Think about your reasons for being in business and your goals for helping clients.
2. A description of your services. This is an opportunity to elaborate on the ways you help your clients.
3. Highlights of the benefits you offer. We recommend limiting your benefits to short phrases or sentences. You may want to use bullet points for each benefit. For example:
   - Over 20 years of experience
   - Full-service firm
4. A history of your firm. Stories describing the birth and growth of your business can make your brochures more interesting to readers.
5. A description of the industries you serve. If you specialize in certain industries, this can give you credibility as having specific expertise.
6. A sample of clients. If your clients permit it, you may want to list their names, and even provide testimonials.

Fact Sheets

Fact sheets are one-page descriptions of your services. They are useful if you offer many services and want to customize your promotional message to prospects with specific needs.

Biographies

Your biography is an opportunity to discuss your expertise, experience, and education. We recommend that you keep it updated with information about speeches you have given, articles you have written, community involvement, and membership in organizations. We also recommend including a current photograph.

Testimonials

An effective technique for building trust is to offer testimonials from satisfied clients. The more recognizable the client names to your targets the better.

We recommend that you ask your clients to provide testimonial letters that you can use for your prospects. A lot of professionals are unsure of how to ask for testimonials. They are reluctant to impose on their valued clients.

A good time to ask is when a client compliments the service that you have provided. You could say something along the lines of, "Thank you for that compliment. May I use that comment in a testimonial?" You can often stimulate compliments by doing client reviews or conducting client satisfaction surveys as we discuss in Skill Module 5. Note: If you are a lawyer and decide to use testimonials, make sure that you comply with the Model Rules of Professional Conduct.

Articles

As we mentioned earlier, articles are an effective way of documenting your expertise. In fact, they are better than brochures for communicating credibility. Whereas brochures are a self-proclamation of value, articles provide value in the form of education. They substantiate your knowledge by allowing people to experience it. And if published, articles give you third party endorsement. See tips for writing and publishing articles in Skill Module 3.

Newsletters

One of your goals in selling is to maintain a consistent, positive presence in your targets' minds. Newsletters give you a valid reason to stay in touch with people. Current software packages make creating beautifully designed newsletters easy and affordable.

Of course, there are many obstacles to newsletters. As with articles, it can be hard to think of important and timely topics. The also require an investment of time to write.

Here are some tips for writing newsletters:

1. Don't be over-ambitious. Some people think that you have to publish a newsletter every week or month. A newsletter once every six months, or once a year, may be sufficient to maintain a positive presence. And, your newsletters don't have to be lengthy. They can be a few paragraphs or a page.

2. Keep a newsletter idea file. If you write down ideas over the course of a year as you notice them, this will help you when it comes time to write your newsletter.
3. Hire professional writers. As with articles, you can hire writers to interview you or your partners, and create well-written newsletters that incorporate your ideas.

The Tools of Your Trade

If you use tools in your practice that help you provide excellent service, then these tools may serve as promotional documents. For example, if you use checklists to ensure accuracy and efficiency, showing your checklists to prospects may be a way of substantiating the value that you offer.

Credibility Kits

A credibility kit is a term that we have coined to describe a collection of several of the promotional documents described above. You can insert promotional documents into a folder with pockets. In this way, you reveal many snapshots of credibility.

A credibility kit can be customized for each prospect. And, as you develop new ideas for promotional information, you can inexpensively change your kit.

You can either purchase pre-made folders from an office supply store, or create your own design with different shapes, sizes, colors, and textures. You can print your logo on it, or any other designs that are appropriate.

In our business, we wanted our credibility kit to be interactive, so we designed a unique clasp. Because our logo is two hands shaking, each side of the clasp is one hand. To open it, you unclasp the two hands. The first thing that many people do after opening it is to play with it by clasping and unclasping the handshake.

You can also be creative about what you place inside the kit. You can insert anything that both fits in the pockets and creates a credibility snapshot. For example, all of the documents listed above can be incorporated into your credibility kit.

You can even insert little gifts. We used to insert letter openers with our logo on them.

And, you can customize how you display the inserts. For example, in our brochure, the articles are layered so that you can see the names of each publication at a glance.

See Exhibit F: Photo of our credibility kit.

Exhibit F—Example of a Credibility Package

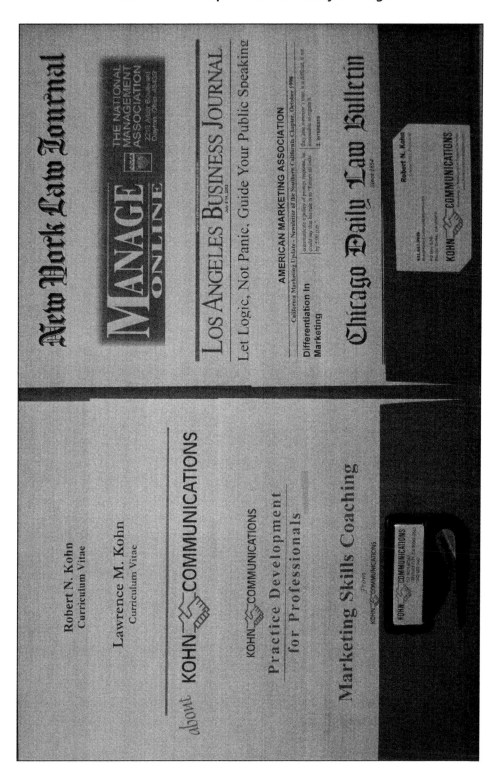

Web Sites

Web sites have become one of the most effective mediums for documenting the value that you offer. They are a safe and convenient medium in which people can learn about your services. Prospects can access information at their leisure and in private.

Like a credibility kit, a Web site gives you the ability to provide a lot of information about your ability to offer value. You can post service descriptions, firm history, philosophy of business, biographies, highlights, testimonials, articles, newsletters, and the tools of your trade. But, because of the electronic medium, you have the ability to do much more.

Here are some tips for creating effective Web sites:

Tip 1: Provide Useful Content

The most important characteristic of a quality Web site is useful content. The more valuable the content, the more people will stay at your site, return to it, and recommend it to their contacts.

Education

A Web site is well suited to providing education. In addition to articles and newsletters, you can provide audio and video seminars. If members of your firm speak or give seminars, you can post a calendar of upcoming events. You may even want to provide links to other sites that are informative.

Interactive tools

If you have tools that your clients and prospects can use in their businesses or personal lives, you may want to post them on your Web site. For example, we know a loan broker who has a tool for computing mortgage payments on his Web site. You type in the loan amount and interest rate and it gives you a monthly payment. If you are a lawyer, make sure that you provide the necessary disclaimers to avoid the possibility of unintentionally forming a lawyer-client relationship.

Tip 2: Make It Easy to Use

Another quality of an effective Web site is simplicity. While more and more people are becoming comfortable with the Internet, most people still appreciate a site that is easy to navigate. Ask your designer to design the tool bar so that it is easy to find and understand. Make sure that all pages on your site can be easily accessed from every other page, and that all links function properly. And, make sure that the site loads quickly. The larger and more complex the site, the longer it may take for it to load on someone's computer.

Make it easy to contact you. And, if you plan on sending newsletters or other information to your contacts, make it easy for people to join your email list. You may even create a button that allows your targets to easily refer your site to their contacts.

Make sure that the Web site pages are designed for printing. We have seen many sites that display photos or information on the screen that are not printable on an 8 1/2-inch sheet of paper. Consider having print buttons on each page that properly format pages for printing.

Exhibit G displays our Web site as an example of many of the above features. (It's a picture of the Web site home page with buttons.)

Tip 3: Explore the Design Technology

Web sites are extremely versatile. Design elements can flash, change color, move around the screen, and make sound. These design elements can be entertaining and capture attention.

However, don't fall into the trap of using every design element just because you can. Adding too many elements to a site can make it confusing and difficult to use.

Keep in mind that different people use different Internet providers and software which display Web sites differently. Your designer may want to use an exiting new Web site design method that works on your screen, but doesn't load or display properly on older computers. Make sure that your Web designer works with fonts, colors, and other design elements that are widely used.

Tip 4: Make Your Web Site Visible to Search Engines

One of the goals of a Web site is to attract strangers who are surfing the Web in search of someone with your services. Your goal is to optimize your site's visibility to search engines. There are a lot of books and articles published on this subject. However, the techniques search engines use to locate Web sites are continually evolving. Make sure that you find Web site designers and consultants who are knowledgeable in the latest search parameters used by search engines.

Search engines currently use algorithms that take into account the following issues:

- Registration with search engines
- The software incorporated into your site design
- The meta-tags or key words that people would use to find your services
- The words that are used within your site
- Advertising on search engines
- The number of other sites that link to your site
- The frequency that your site is updated
- The number of times your site is viewed

Exhibit G—Example of a Web Site

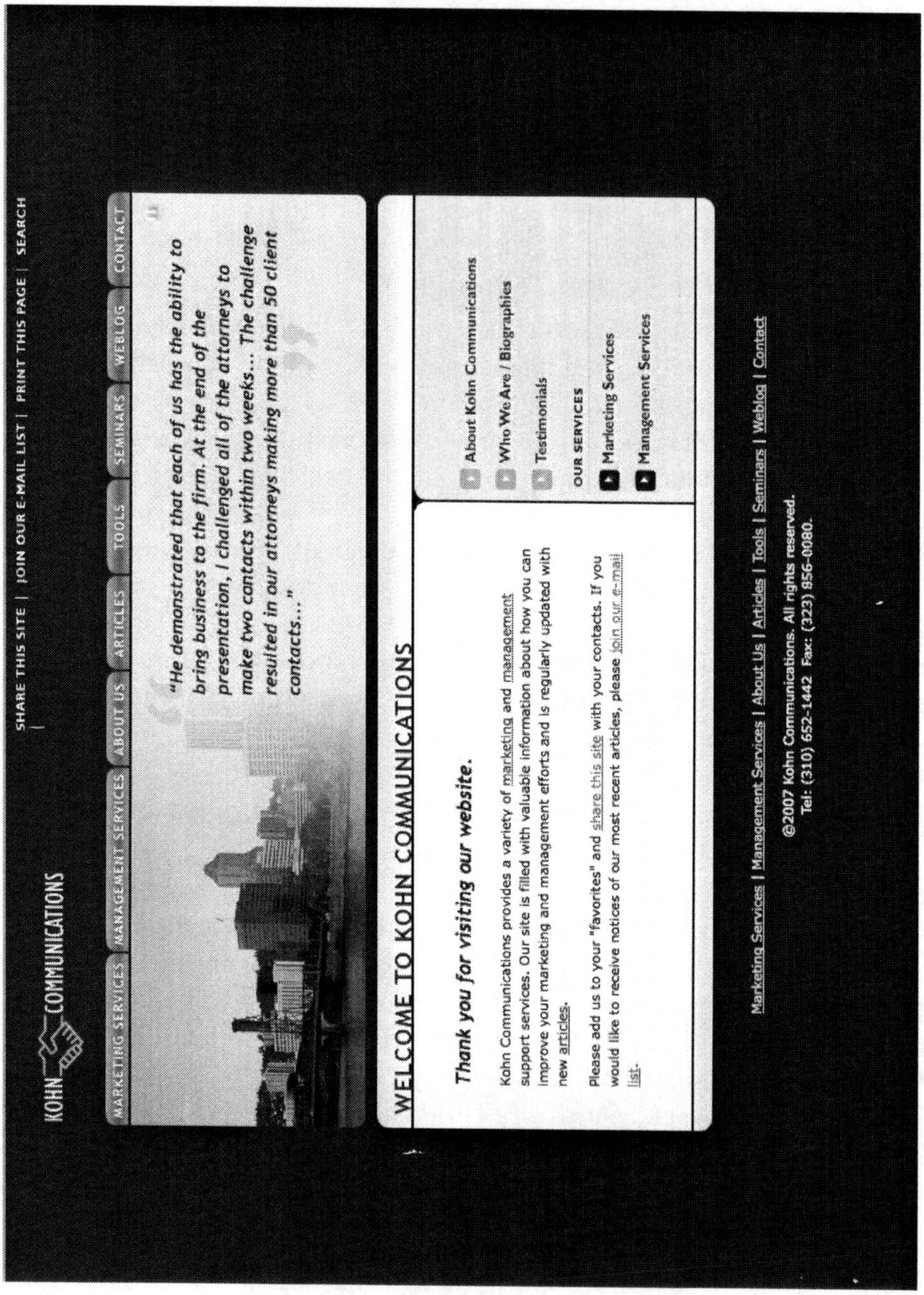

Tip 5: Send Email Announcements

An effective way of driving traffic to your site is to send emails to your contact list inviting them to visit your site. For example, when you add something to your site, such as an article, newsletter, or seminar, you can send an email announcement with an imbedded link to your site. When people click on the link, they are instantly taken to the place on your site where they can see the item you are announcing. Once there, they can visit other areas of your site.

Tip 6: Create a Web Log

Another technique that may help drive traffic to your site is to create a Web log (or Blog.) Web logs are a type of Web site allowing you to post information on specific topics whenever you want, and the public has the ability to post their comments. Since it can be updated frequently, this may be a factor in helping search engines to locate your Web log. Since you can cross-reference your Web site, having a Web log may help to drive traffic to your Web site.

Web logs are generally easy to create and your Web site designer should know how to set one up. But, maintaining them on an ongoing basis requires a commitment of time. If there are several people in your organization, you may be able to share the responsibility of updating information.

Incorporate Your Promotional Documents into Your Discussion

Too often after handing someone a brochure, or giving out a Web site address, professionals rely on the prospect to review the material. Unfortunately, people get busy or they lose interest. So, you should take steps to insure that people actually review the information.

Use the brochure as a talking paper

When you hand out your brochure, instead of simply giving it to someone, we suggest that you review it with them. Point out the various sections and what they say. In this way, your prospects are sure to see all of the relevant information.

Use your site as a slide show

An effective way of using your Web site is to ask people to look at your site while you are talking with them on the phone. Give them a tour of the site. Tell them which pages to look at and show them the value that it offers.

This participation helps prospects explore your site in depth and gain a better appreciation of the value that you offer. It also prepares them to describe your services to other decision-makers at their companies.

Conclusion

Your documents are an integral part of the selling process. Make sure that your documents create snapshots of credibility. In addition to describing how you offer value, whenever possible, provide value-in-advance as a way of substantiating the value that you offer.

Tips for Client Satisfaction Surveys

CLIENT SATISFACTION SURVEYS are an important tool in your selling effort. They help you to strengthen client loyalty and generate more business. However, as with all of the techniques mentioned in this book, there are many obstacles to conducting surveys.

Fear of Receiving Criticism

Asking your clients to evaluate the quality of your work and services exposes you to potential criticism. And, nobody likes to hear criticism. But, the cost of losing a client should far outweigh the discomfort of negative feedback. Learning of a client's dissatisfaction may help you salvage the relationship before it is too late.

The Assumption That You Know Your Clients' Attitudes

Because you are working with a client you may make the assumption that you are aware of your client's attitudes. In fact, many professionals are surprised to learn that clients were not as satisfied as expected. There is often a disconnect between professionals and their clients with regard to service. Clients may not be good at voicing grievances. As a result, dissatisfied clients often leave without explaining why. So, even if you are certain that your clients are satisfied, it is still a good idea to conduct surveys.

If you learn that your clients are completely satisfied, then it is still a positive experience for you and the client. It feels good to receive compliments. And it gives satisfied clients an opportunity to articulate their feelings. This reinforces their loyalty and makes them proud that they have selected you as their provider. Furthermore, when clients describe what you do well, it crafts their dialogue in describing your services to others.

Even when clients are fully satisfied, they still may need additional services that you or people you know could be providing. So, a survey is an effective tool for discovering needs.

Concern That You Appear Weak

A lot of professionals are reluctant to conduct surveys because they are concerned about appearing weak. Quite to the contrary, we believe they make you appear strong. Conducting surveys is a sign of integrity, faith in the value that you offer, and concern for the well-being of your clients.

Conducting surveys also help you to increase your confidence in the value that you offer. The process of crafting survey questions helps you gain greater clarity about the value that you want your clients to appreciate. For example, how responsive, organized, and efficient are you? Do you really offer a good deal as we described in Chapter 4?

The Fear of Imposing

Some people express concern that surveys could potentially annoy clients. They impose on your clients' time and they might be perceived as merely a superficial attempt to sell additional services. With regard to your imposing on their time, most of the clients we know welcome surveys. They pay their providers a lot of money and understand that surveys help to ensure quality service.

With regard to the fear that it will be perceived as a sales effort, we recommend that you limit the survey to services provided. Don't mention other services you could offer.

It is true that surveys are a sales tool. As mentioned earlier, their purpose is to increase client loyalty and generate more business. But, they can be an indirect sales tool. If done properly, you can use surveys to bond with your clients and gather information that will help you improve the quality of service. Once clients indicate that they are satisfied, you can take steps later to discuss additional services or the possibility of getting referrals.

Client Satisfaction Surveys

There are three types of surveys:

1. In-person
2. Telephone, and
3. Written

There are advantages and disadvantages to each.

In person

In-person surveys allow the greatest insight into your clients' attitudes. They are an opportunity for bonding and reinforcing relationships.

However, they are also more costly and time consuming, especially if your clients are not local. Because of this, in-person surveys should be reserved for your most important clients. These include:

- Your largest clients
- Clients with the most opportunities for growth
- Clients who are well connected to potential referral sources.

Phone

Phone surveys conducted are less expensive and time consuming, and easier to schedule. They can also be delegated to a staff person or an off-site company that specializes in conducting surveys. But, it is harder to detect emotion over the phone than in person. And, if they are conducted by other people, you lose the bonding experience.

Written

With a written survey, you provide a questionnaire via mail, email, or on the Web. These require the least amount of time and they are good for getting data from large numbers of clients. But, they also have the lowest response rate.

Tips for Conducting Effective Client Satisfaction Surveys

Once you decide to conduct a survey, here are some tips for maximizing your success.

Tip 1: Script Your Request to Conduct a Survey

A lot of professionals do not know how to bring up the subject of doing a survey. We recommend that you script your dialogue in advance. Here are two suggestions:

1. We regularly conduct surveys for our clients and we would like your input.
2. Now that we have worked together for a while, we think it might be a good idea to get your feedback about the quality of our services.

Tip 2: Craft Questions That Reflect the Value That You Offer

One of the greatest benefits of surveys is that they help you become clear about the value that you offer. The greater this clarity, the more confident you will feel about promoting your services and the easier it will be to communicate that value to your targets. So, use the survey process as a technique for brainstorming all of the ways that you offer value. Refer to Chapter 4 for examples of the benefits that you offer.

Tip 3: Don't Sell

Don't be overt in asking for new business or referrals. Don't discuss other services. The risk is being perceived as insincere or deceptive. Rather, think of your survey as an indirect sales tool. Ask questions genuinely designed to capture your clients' feelings and beliefs. For example, "How would you rate us in meeting deadlines?" Or, "How would you rate us on understanding your needs?" Clients will appreciate that these questions reveal your intent to insure that you are providing value. Refer to Exhibit H—Sample Client Satisfaction Survey by Phone.

Tip 4: Ask Clients to Elaborate

For scores to be meaningful, they require an explanation. When clients give a low score, ask clients to elaborate. Ask for examples. Ask what it would take to increase the score. Even if a score is high, you may want a client to describe why. This reinforces their good feelings and gives you things to talk about with other prospects.

Tip 5: Have Clarity before Moving on

Make sure that you clearly understand the client's response. If you are unclear what the client really means, ask them to provide an example. Or, rephrase what they are saying. For example, you could say, "I want to make sure I understand what you mean. What I hear you saying is . . ."

Tip 6: Respond Quickly to Negative Feedback

If you receive negative feedback, call or meet with the client to discuss a plan to correct the problem. Clarify their perception and then negotiate changes.

Tip 7: Build on Positive Feedback

Receiving positive feedback may be an opportunity to ask for testimonials, discuss additional issues, and ask for referrals.

Exhibit H—Sample Client Satisfaction Survey by Phone

CLIENT NAME: (omitted)

DATE OF SURVEY: (omitted)

INTERVIEWER'S ASSESSMENTS: Mr. (client's name) returned my call and was immediately available to do the survey. He acknowledged that he has had a long-standing quality relationship with your firm. This survey reveals a significant opportunity for your firm to enhance and expand your relationship with Mr. (client's name) by
  1.) heeding his suggestion to "sit down" and redefine the relationship, and
  2.) accepting his offer to consider any additional services that your firm could provide.

THE SURVEY:
On a scale of 1 to 10… 10 being the best…

Question:
1. How would you rate (name of firm) on understanding your needs?

Response: **7**
"We've had a long relationship. Sometimes I think when you work with the same company for so many years, you just keep things operating the same. I think it would be useful if they reassessed our needs. I would recommend their interviewing us, asking what our concerns and our needs are. Just asking, checking in beyond the work that we already do together would be helpful."

Question:
2. How would you rate (name of firm) with regard to the quality of advice you receive?

Response: **8**
"In terms of being able to quote specific policies and the law, I think they are good at that. For the most part, the advice I get from their people is very practical. But, I feel that they could still do a better job of relating that to our specific business needs."

Question:
3. How would you evaluate their ability to meet deadlines?

Response: **9**
"They do a good job of laying out what time frames they plan to stick to. They're also good at accommodating last-minute scheduling needs."

Question:
4. How would you rate (name of firm)'s responsiveness to your needs?

Exhibit H—Sample Client Satisfaction Survey by Phone—(*Continued*)

Response: **9**
"They are very responsive. Whenever I leave them a voice message or email, I know that I'll be contacted right away. I appreciate that."

Question:
5.   Is there anything you would like (name of firm) to be doing that they are not doing now?

Response:
"It might be an improvement to be given an estimate of what their services would cost. Their bills sometimes surprise me. Especially because we deal with them on a monthly basis, providing us estimates would help our financial planning. It would be a benefit."

Question:
6.   How do you perceive the value that you're receiving from (name of firm)?

Response: **10**
"I deal with four different firms. On a comparative basis, (name of firm) is the top. They are very competitive in terms of the cost of their services. "

Question:
7.   How do you rate the firm's energy and determination in pursing your goals?

Response: **8**
"It would be great to do more planning together. To review; What is our relationship? What am I providing them and what are they providing me? What else could we do together? There may be other services they could provide us. The person we had been dealing with at (name of firm) left a year ago, and now we are dealing with another person, who is fine. But that transition was rocky for us at first and I think it would be helpful if we just sat down together to review and plan."

Question:
8.   What are the areas where you would like to see improvement in (name of firm)'s work for you?

Response:
"Sometimes their billing is a bit obscure. It's not so much that it's vague; it's very detailed. But it's unclear the way it's presented exactly what the given task relates to. Other than my earlier comments, I have no other feedback. Generally I am very happy with their firm."

Always strike while the iron is hot. When a client compliments your service, you might respond, "May I use that comment for prospects?" Or, "I am glad that you feel that way. We also value having you as a client, and maybe we could spend some time discussing additional ways that we may be of service."

Tip 8: Use a Client Survey Checklist

Being organized will help in your follow-up efforts. Use the checklist like the one we have illustrated in Exhibit I, the client satisfaction survey checklist, to make sure that you are clear about your follow-up strategy and the steps taken to implement it.

Conclusion

Surveys are an effective method for revealing problems, building trust and loyalty, and stimulating new work. Don't be afraid of criticism. Rather, think of surveys as an opportunity to strengthen relationships and build your own confidence in the value that you offer.

Exhibit I—Client Satisfaction Survey Checklist

(Check List)

Client Name: _____   **Billing Partner:** _____

Obtained approval from client: ___ /___ /___

Scheduled survey on: ___ /___ /___

Conducted survey on: ___ /___ /___

Discussed survey results with billing partner and identified follow-up strategy:

_____

_____

_____

_____

_____

_____

_____

_____

_____

_____

_____

_____

_____

_____

_____

_____

_____

_____

_____

_____

_____

_____

_____

Completed: ___ /___ /___

Implemented follow-up: ___ /___ /___

Comfortable Techniques for Working a Room

IN THE SELLING PROCESS, you may find yourself at a social function where it is necessary to "work the room." The more people you meet, the more likely you are to develop new business. So, it makes sense to attend events that can provide you with an opportunity to meet quality targets.

However, you may find working-a-room situations to be distasteful. You may feel shy or awkward about mingling with strangers. You may feel an obligation to appear witty or clever.

But, these obstacles can be overcome through specific techniques that we teach. When you go to an event and find yourself in a sea of strangers, here are some tips to make the experience more safe and effective.

Tip 1: Do Research

One of the reasons you may find working a room distasteful is that you are assuming that your goal is to sell. You may believe that you have to be charming and entertaining. However, this notion of working a room is a myth. It is unrealistic to think that you could meet someone for the first time at an event and convince them to hire you on the spot. Potential prospects you meet may not have an immediate need for your services, or they may already have a relationship with another provider.

Rather, you should think of working a room as research. Your

> ▼
>
> Thinking of it as research, not selling, will make working-a-room a more pleasurable and worthwhile experience.

163

job is to meet people and ask questions. The focus should be on learning about the people you meet. It's no secret that people love to talk about themselves. If you can provide an opportunity for someone to discuss their needs and interests, not only will they appreciate you, but you will eliminate the burden of having to be witty and clever. Furthermore, you can learn important information about their needs. This will help you identify quality targets that may be worth staying in touch with. Thinking of it as research, not selling, will make working a room a more pleasurable and worthwhile experience.

Tip 2: Target Who You Want to Meet

Another obstacle to working a room is that you may go to events without considering who else will be attending. You may have already had experiences in which you went to a poorly targeted networking event and came away with a bunch of business cards from people that are unlikely to hire you. These experiences reinforce your belief that working a room is a waste of time and discourage you from trying again.

The way to overcome this obstacle is by targeting and knowing in advance precisely who you want to meet. Imagine if you were to invest the same time and effort in a room full of quality prospects and referral sources. For example, if you were a CPA and found yourself in a room full of bankers or business owners, it would be an extremely rewarding experience, even if you met only a small percentage of individuals.

Refer to Chapter 8 for some helpful tips on targeting quality events. Begin by asking your clients and referral sources what organizations they belong to. They may even agree to bring you to one of their functions and introduce you to their colleagues. As you meet people, ask them what other organizations they support. You will find that in a relatively short period of time you will learn about a vast array of charitable, civic, community, religious, business, trade, and professional groups that will provide a fertile supply of prospects and referral sources for you to meet.

Tip 3: Find Networking Events That Provide Opportunities to Interact

Not all programs are well suited for meeting your targets. Some programs are purely educational in nature. For example, if you go to a seminar in which the audience is situated in rows all facing the front of the room in school-room fashion, it may be difficult to meet anyone. If your goal is to meet people, attend programs that provide interaction such as receptions before and afterwards, dinner tables at which you face each other. In fact, if time is limited you may only want to attend the networking portions of events and not stay for the speech.

Tip 4: Arrive Early

You will find that it is easier to make acquaintances when the room is relatively empty. It is much more difficult to meet people after they have already formed small groups. Furthermore, if you arrive late, you may miss valuable interaction opportunities.

Tip 5: Meet the Staff

Upon arrival, introduce yourself to the organization's staff. They will know many of the members of the organization and will be glad to introduce you to appropriate targets.

Tip 6: Go with a Friend

Going with someone can ease the pressure of being alone in a room full of strangers. You can work as a team to meet people. When you meet a potential prospect, you might offer to introduce that person to your colleague. But avoid the temptation of sticking together for the entire event. Make a pact before you enter to work individually. If the function is for a meal, avoid sitting at the same table. Your goal is to meet others, not socialize with your teammate.

Tip 7: Stimulate Meaningful Conversation

Meeting people is only an initial step. Your next objective is to develop rapport. This requires engaging people in conversation.

A significant obstacle in working a room is that you may feel frustrated with the superficial nature of the conversations. One solution to this problem is to talk about issues that are important to the people you meet. Ask about the issues affecting their businesses. How are current economic trends or politics affecting their businesses? These types of questions may also help you identify needs.

Tip 8: Go for Volume

As you meet and interact with people, you may be lulled into the risk of getting comfortable with one or two friendly individuals. Be careful not to limit yourself. Rather, go for volume and meet as many people as possible. The more contacts you make now, brief as they may be, the more potential relationships you may pursue in the future.

Tip 9: Get the Card

Once you've met someone who you have identified as a quality prospect, make sure that you ask for their business card. You may even want to make notes on the card reminding you about each person and the topic of your conversation. And of course, add all qualified targets to your mailing list.

Tip 10: Follow Up

A lack of follow up minimizes the value of meeting someone. We recommend that you make a commitment as you engage in conversation to implement some future activity. Too often, professionals ask for a business card with the intention of following up, but never follow through. Making a commitment, such as promising to mail something or call to schedule a meeting, forces you to take action. When you follow through, it demonstrates to your prospect that you are someone who fulfills promises by keeping commitments. And, it increases the likelihood of doing business.

Conclusion

Working a room can be an important part of your sales effort. Effectively implemented, it's a way to meet new people and build closer relationships with existing contacts.

And while it may at first appear to be an unpleasant experience, with some practice, many professionals actually find it fun as well as financially rewarding.

Tips for Time Management

A COMMON OBSTACLE TO SELLING is lack of time. When you are busy, it may seem impossible to incorporate selling into your schedule.

The purpose of this skill module is to give you some time management tips. But, before we do, make sure that lack of time is really the obstacle. As we pointed out in Chapter 2, lack of time is often an excuse to avoid selling. People typically allow their discomfort to cloud their thinking. If a task is unpleasant or unfamiliar it's easy to feel too busy to address it. So, review the reasons for discomfort in Chapter 2 before concluding that lack of time is the only reason for your reluctance to sell.

If after reviewing the obstacles, you are convinced that lack of time *is* the primary reason for your lack of attention to selling, then you may need to improve your time management skills. Selling is too important to be neglected.

Here are some time management tips:

1. Limit interruptions
2. Evaluate the priority of tasks
3. Avoid the black holes
4. Minimize clutter in your work space
5. Invest your selling time wisely
6. Delegate effectively

Tip 1: Limit Interruptions

Professionals are often reactive. You may be in the habit of taking every phone call from your clients, or responding every time a co-worker knocks on your door. Interruptions are time-consuming because they require refocusing. Instead, set aside time for projects. Commit blocks of time when you will not be interrupted. Don't confuse good service with unnecessary interruptions. Even the most demanding clients and co-workers understand that you have other issues to handle.

> Don't confuse good service with unnecessary interruptions.

Tip 2: Evaluate the Priority of Tasks

Different tasks have different levels of priority. And, not all tasks require your attention. Always strive to work on tasks that are the most profitable use of your time. Each time you consider a task ask yourself whether you should discard, defer, delegate, or do the task.

Tip 3: Avoid Black Holes

People often invest the most time in the least valuable activities. Start paying attention to the black holes in your life that consume your time and energy.

Individuals who waste your time

Think of your worst clients. They often require a lot of your time and squabble over every invoice. Think about problem employees who never respond to your motivational efforts and fill your life with aggravation. Recognize these individuals and have the courage to terminate your relationships with them.

Conversations that waste time

Often, the fear of appearing rude causes you to get trapped in conversations with co-workers and friends when you are busy. One way to save time without rudeness is to tell a person at the beginning of your conversation that you have only five minutes to talk. Notifying people of time limitations helps them get down to the meat of a meeting. It's a way of cutting them off without putting them down.

Another technique is to stand as you talk with another person. Your body language does not offer the other person a chance to sit down. Too often people unwittingly sit down and get comfortable, enjoying their coffee or playing with that magnetic sculpture on you desk. A "standing meeting" is usually a shorter meeting.

Promote brevity. If you enjoy speaking ad nauseam, you set a low standard for your employees. Keep your words (both spoken and written) to a minimum and require the same of others.

Thoughts and feelings that waste time

Negative thoughts and feelings often waste your time and energy. A common culprit is worry. For many people, worry feels like a response to a problem. For example, worrying about a test feels like a motivator to study. But, there is a huge difference between thinking about an issue and worrying. Worry focuses on anxiety. Worry clouds thinking and slows it down. It can produce irrational responses, which take time to repair. Stress from worry can cause illness, which wastes more time. It can even cause a heart attack and kill you—the ultimate time waster. Worry is a habit that can be difficult to break. If you learn to consider risks and not suffer form the anxiety of worry, you'll be better at solving problems, feel happier, and save lots of time.

Become aware of all of the negative thoughts and feelings that consume your time such as jealousy, self-pity, bitterness, blame, shame, remorse, guilt, prejudice, and many more. Listen to your inner voice and decide if the messages you're hearing are promoting a good use of time or wasting it.

> ▼
> Avoid negative thoughts and feeling that sap your time and energy.

Tip 4: Minimize Clutter in Your Work Space

A messy office is an inefficient office. Files get lost. Papers end up in the wrong files. People who need access to documents can't find them. From a client relations perspective, when clients see a messy office, it reveals a lack of organization and could erode their confidence.

Messy professionals usually justify piles of files as a visual "to-do" list. But, that visual stimulation actually wastes time because the files act as distracting "mental magnets."

If you have a problem with clutter, consider adding a couple of filing cabinets to your office. If you need a visual reminder, try technology. Electronic organizers and software packages can really help.

You might want to consider keeping every project in a separate file. Create a cover sheet with a list of tasks and deadlines. This is an efficient way of remembering what is happening on each project and what needs to be done.

Tip 5: Invest Your Selling Time Wisely

Since you don't have a lot of time for selling, whatever time you *do* invest should be used wisely. Review the chapters of this book to find activities that you believe are the most safe and effective.

For example, invest in good targets (Chapter 5). Speed up the sales cycle by revealing your interest in doing business (Chapter 7). Create efficient systems for staying in touch with your targets (Chapter 9).

Delegate sales-related tasks to your staff. For example, enlist the support of your staff to find out the approval procedures of your prospects (Chapter 7); research organizations for speaking opportunities (Chapter 8); develop a mailing list (Chapter 9).

Schedule time for selling

Schedule blocks of time for selling tasks such as writing an article or doing some targeting. Once you identify an activity that you have faith in, commit a specific amount of time. For example, reserve twenty minutes in the morning or on a weekend to work on an outline for an article. Schedule a few minutes each day for thinking about selling or making phone calls. We recommend reserving these times in your calendar. When you reserve time for priorities, it is easier to squeeze them into your day.

▼
Use your calendar to schedule time for selling.

Decide on a time to stop a task, too. A tight limit on the time to implement something makes an unpleasant task easier to start. It also increases the likelihood that you will use the time effectively.

Do your selling tasks first

Many selling tasks don't require much time. You can spend more time worrying about selling tasks than actually doing them. Calling someone to schedule lunch may take only a few minutes. But, it could take months to make the call if you keep putting it off. Then you waste time each time you think about it. We recommend doing selling tasks first thing in the morning. Get them out of the way before concentrating on more comfortable tasks.

Leave messages that further the process

Your goal in selling is to maintain a consistent positive presence in the lives of your targets. You don't always need to have lengthy meetings. Much of your selling can be done with brief email or voice-mail messages.

Email and voice-mail are particularly effective for scheduling activities. If you are trying to schedule a lunch with someone who is hard to get a hold of, instead playing voice tag, leave some options. For example, "I can give you three options for our next meeting: the 12th at noon or the 14th or the 20th. Please choose a date or leave me a message with other options that work for you later in the month."

Tip 6: Delegate Effectively

Delegation is an effective time management technique, which frees up your time to develop business and build client relationships.

Of course, there are obstacles to delegation. You may not believe that you can delegate effectively. You may even have had negative experiences with it. But, don't let your negative voice convince that you can't delegate. Provided that you see its value, you can improve your ability to delegate. You can develop your systems, habits, and skills.

Here are several reasons our clients give for not delegating, and some techniques for overcoming these obstacles:

"I don't have someone to delegate to."

Problem: You may be self-employed and work alone. Or, you may work in a company, but everyone is busy. Or, you may not have the authority to delegate.

Solution: There are only two possible solutions to this problem.

1. Hire someone. If you have a small budget, consider hiring part-time staff. Many of our solo-practitioner clients use part-time employees, some of whom even work at home.
2. Lobby for support. You may be able to convince your colleagues that your ability to delegate would be more profitable for everyone, especially if you can use your time to generate new business.

"By the time I explain a task to someone, I could do it myself."

Problem: It may seem like it takes more time to teach someone how to do a task, than simply doing it yourself.

Solution: Delegation is a skill that must be learned by both parties. The key is to create systems that insure that quality information and accurate expectations of the quality standards are communicated to the delagatee. Inadequate information and expectations cause errors. And, errors waste time.

Use the task management form.
While it is easy to blame the delagatee for not doing a good job, poor quality delegation is often the fault of the delegator. To help you improve delegation, we created a form called the "Task Manager" (Exhibit J). The Task Manager ensures that the delagatee has all of the necessary information and expectations to do the job well. It forces you to be clear about your task description, required resources for completing the job, your specific quality standards, and your timeline. The form can be filled out either by you, or by delagatee.

Exhibit J—Task Manager

Name: _____

Date Received: _____ **Deadline: (Date)** _____ **(Time)** _____

Task Description: _____
_____

Required Resources: _____
_____

Loop List: _____ _____ _____
_____ _____ _____

Quality Standards: _____
_____
_____
_____

TIMELINE

Interim Steps	Deadline	Completed
_____	_____	_____
_____	_____	_____
_____	_____	_____
_____	_____	_____
_____	_____	_____
_____	_____	_____
_____	_____	_____
_____	_____	_____
_____	_____	_____
_____	_____	_____
_____	_____	_____

Create a checklist for repetitive tasks.

The first time you delegate a task, we recommend that you also delegate the creation of a job checklist. In this way, you are creating a manual for future delegation.

Problem: Some types of jobs, such as non-repetitive activities may not be suitable for delegation.

Solution: You have to consider whether it is in your interest to be offering non-repetitive services. Or, charge a premium for them because they are so time consuming and not delegable.

> *"There isn't anyone here who I trust*
> *to do the work as well as I do it."*

Problem: Many professionals don't have confidence in their staff.

Solution: Begin with small tasks. For example, if the job is to write an article, you might have the person draft an outline, and then get back to you. You can't build trust over night. It could take years of discussion and experience and results. Even when someone is bright and well-spoken, you still may not have confidence in his or her ability. You have to take a long-term view. But, if you don't start now, then you will never be able to achieve significant growth.

The alternative is to hire someone at a much higher level where you'll have immediate confidence. However, it could be expensive to hire someone at this level.

> *"My clients always ask for me and would be*
> *disappointed if I delegated the work."*

Problem: You have taught your clients that you are always going to do the work. So, they expect you to do it.

Solution: Sell your team. Explain to your clients that it is in their best interests to have your team member do the work because it will save them money. Jobs handled by a junior person can be billed at a lower rate. And, it will free up your time to more creatively apply your expertise and guidance.

Build your clients' confidence in your team members by introducing them to your clients. Bring your team members into client meetings early in the process so that they understand the issues from inception. Teach your delagatees how to interact with clients. They need to be assertive by asking questions and giving their opinions.

> *"I am afraid to lose control over the client."*

Problem: There is the risk that your delagatee will bond with the client and steal these relationships.

Solution: Stay connected with your clients. Maintain the supervisory position. Engage in social interaction which is fun and effective for maintaining the relationship.

Conclusion

While you may be busy, don't convince yourself that you don't have the time to sell. You can always make time for priorities. You may have to change your habits and routines. You may have to learn time management and delegations skills. But, if you invest some time and energy now in developing these habits and skills, it will free up time in the future for you to build your practice and do more of the things that you enjoy.

Tips on Creating an Achievable Strategic Plan

IF YOU HAVE READ all of the preceding chapters and Skill Modules, then by now you should have a greater feeling of comfort with selling. And, you should have a clearer understanding of selling strategies, including why they work and how to implement them. You should be ready to develop a strategic plan for your selling effort.

It makes sense that you write down the tasks that you want to implement. Organization facilitates implementation. But, keep in mind that planning alone does not alter behavior. If you want to be successful in your selling effort, then you need to take action. The difference is in the doing. So, it is important that you create a strategic plan that is achievable.

In Exhibit K, we have given you a strategic plan worksheet to help you create an achievable plan. It asks you to document your current status as you begin your effort. Then, it asks you to make choices about safe and effective strategies that you are willing to explore.

Here are some tips to help you create your plan:

Tip 1: Don't Bite off More than You Can Chew

Don't pick too many tasks. It can be overwhelming. You don't have to overhaul your life. Rather, you can gradually implement strategies and in time, develop new habits and a way of thinking. We recommend picking tasks that you can complete in a 30-day period or less. Consider how much time you realistically have to commit to selling and chose tasks that are achievable.

If you only have time to schedule a lunch with one or two people in a 30-day period, then commit to one or two lunches. But, keep your commitment.

If you are working on a large project such as writing an article, break it down into smaller steps. For example, commit ten minutes one day for starting an outline, another ten minutes on another day to write the introductory paragraph, and keep committing increments of time until the project is complete.

Some projects are long-term such as getting speaking engagements. Again, break it down into the incremental steps. Spend a little time doing some research, and at another time, start contacting the organizations.

Your strategic plan should map out not only what you are going to do but when you can realistically get to each step in the process. Use your calendar to decide when you will have time to implement specific tasks. Then, reserve that time so that you don't schedule things that interfere with your implementation.

Tip 2: Stay in Your Comfort Zone

Focus on some tasks that you believe are safe and effective. Always do things that you believe are appropriate for your personality, and that you genuinely believe are a practical use of your time and money. The rule is: If something is uncomfortable, don't do it. Pushing outside of your comfort zone will make you reluctant to take action.

But, just because one type of strategy feels uncomfortable, don't give yourself permission to give up altogether. Challenge your beliefs about strategies that you find uncomfortable. As we pointed out in Chapter 2, you may be holding prejudices that are not valid. But, if it turns out that your feelings about a particular strategy *are* valid, keep looking for other ideas. This book is filled with examples of safe and effective selling strategies.

Keep in mind that as you practice selling strategies and begin experiencing success, your comfort zone should expand. You will feel more comfortable trying new strategies that previously you may not have considered. But for now, focus on things that are within your comfort zone.

Tip 3: Document the Benefits That You Offer

As we mentioned in Chapter 4, the more confident you are in the value that you offer, the more enthusiastic you will be about selling, and more likely you will be to inspire others to hire you. Review the methods of offering value discussed in Chapter 4 and create a comprehensive list of benefits that you offer.

Tip 4: Select Your Targets Wisely

Business comes from relationships. This means that you need to either nurture existing relationships or meet new people.

Exhibit K—Strategic Selling Plan Worksheet

BEGINNING MEASUREMENTS (To evaluate your future success it is necessary to document your current activities and success)

⁕ **ANNUAL ORIGINATIONS**

How many clients have you originated over the past year?   Number of Clients _____   Amount of Income $: _____

If a team effort, how many clients have you helped to originate over the past year? _____   Amount of Income $: _____

⁕ **CONTACT MANAGEMENT**

Do you have a mailing list?   ☐ Yes   ☐ No   Is it manual or on computer? _____   How many qualified targets are on your list? _____

Are you using a relationship development system?   ☐ Yes   ☐ No   Is it manual or on computer? _____

⁕ **ORGANIZATIONAL INVOLVEMENT**

What organizations are you a member of that provide networking opportunities? _____

Name of organization	Demographics of members	Networking opportunities (committees, public speaking, writing, socializing)
_____	_____	_____
_____	_____	_____
_____	_____	_____

⁕ **ARTICLE WRITING**

How many articles have you written over the past year? _____   How many have been published? _____

⁕ **PUBLIC SPEAKING**

How many speeches have you given over the past year? _____   Have they been effective for meeting qualified targets? ☐ Yes   ☐ No

Have the led to new business?   ☐ Yes   ☐ No

⁕ **ONE-ON-ONE BUSINESS DEVELOPMENT**

How many lunches for business generation purposes do you have in a given week/month/year? _____ / _____ / _____

⁕ **OTHER ACTIVITIES**

Have there been any other current or past business development activities?   ☐ Yes   ☐ No

If yes, describe them: _____ (Attach List)

⁕ **REVIEW PROCESS**

How frequently do you review your business development tasks?   ☐ Randomly   ☐ Daily   ☐ Every few days   ☐ Weekly   ☐ Bi-Monthly   ☐ Monthly

Exhibit K—Strategic Selling Plan Worksheet—(*Continued*)

PLAN (What safe and effective steps will you take to generate new business?)

Create a selling file. ☐ Completed

Document the benefits that you offer: _____

_____ (Attach List)

Which benefits do you want to improve? _____

_____ (Attach List)

Print out a "Capture your observations form" to help you notice and improve the benefits you offer ☐ Completed

✳ TARGETING

Targeting Strategies:

Begin by targeting: ☐ Existing contacts ☐ Strangers ☐ Prospects ☐ Referral sources ☐ Resources

When will you schedule time to begin building your target list? ____ /____ /____ How much time will you schedule? _____

Target List:

Name	Prospect	Referral Source	Resource	Created Relationship Development Worksheet
_____	☐	☐	☐	☐
_____	☐	☐	☐	☐
_____	☐	☐	☐	☐
_____	☐	☐	☐	☐

(Attach List)

Describe your client demographics: _____

_____

_____ (Attach List)

✳ BUILDING YOUR BASE OF CONTACTS

What are your strategies for meeting new people?

☐ Ask your contacts to introduce you to their contacts   ☐ Join or participate in organizations

List the organizations that cater to your targets:

Name of organization	Demographics of members	Networking opportunities (committees, public speaking, writing, socializing)
_____	_____	_____
_____	_____	_____
_____	_____	_____

Reproduced with permission of Kohn Communications (**www.kohncommunications.com**).

Exhibit K—Strategic Selling Plan Worksheet—(*Continued*)

✳ ARTICLE WRITING
Do you want to write an article?

Potential topics	Potential publications	Name of editor
_____	_____	_____
_____	_____	_____
_____	_____	_____
_____	_____	_____

(Attach List)

Will you delegate the task of calling editors? _____ Name of caller: _____

When will you schedule time to work on an article? ____ / ____ / ____ How much time will you schedule? _____

✳ PUBLIC SPEAKING
Do you want to do public speaking?

Potential topics	Potential publications	Name of contact
_____	_____	_____
_____	_____	_____
_____	_____	_____
_____	_____	_____

Will you delegate the task of calling for speaking opportunities? _____ Name of caller: _____

When will you schedule time to work on a speech? ____ / ____ / ____ How much time will you schedule? _____

✳ SEMINARS
Do you want to conduct seminars?

Potential topics
_____
_____

(Attach List)

Where will you conduct them? _____ How many people do you plan to invite? _____

✳ CONTACT SOFTWARE
When will you delegate time to research software? ____ / ____ / ____ How much time will you schedule? _____

List of software programs identified:

Name of program _____ Features _____ Price $ _____ (Attach List)

When will you install software ____ / ____ / ____ When will you begin importing names? ____ / ____ / ____

Will you delegate the process of adding names? ☐ Yes ☐ No Task of adding names will be assigned to: _____

Exhibit K—Strategic Selling Plan Worksheet—(*Continued*)

* **OTHER PROJECTS**

_____

_____

_____

_____

(Attach List)

* **REVIEW PROCESS**

How often will you review your business development tasks? ☐ Daily   ☐ Weekly   ☐ Monthly

Will you be accountable to someone? ☐ Yes   ☐ No   Name of person: _____

How often will you meet? _____

As we stressed in Chapter 5, we always recommend that you begin by targeting the people you already know. Your existing contacts are more accessible. Make a target list of people you know who meet the criteria of qualified prospects, referral sources, or resources.

Tip 5: Fill Out Relationship Development Worksheets

For every important target, fill out a Relationship Development Worksheet shown in Exhibit C in Chapter 9. Remember that selling is a process. Once you have met and qualified your targets, then you need to build trust and credibility by communicating value. The Relationship Development Worksheet will help you feel more connected to your targets, plan your communication strategies, and stay in touch.

Once you decide on a strategy, make sure that you schedule a "do date," and put it in your calendar. Keep your worksheets in a three-ring binder. Later, after you have mastered the skill of using these forms, you can graduate to contact management software.

Tip 6: Leverage Relationships

An effective way of meeting new people is through the people you already know. Look at your targets and identify the names of people you know who you think might have the willingness and the ability to introduce you to new targets. Fill out a Relationship Development Worksheet for each contact and develop comfortable dialogue for asking them for introductions.

Tip 7: Research Organizations

Well-targeted organizations can be a safe and effective way of meeting new people. To find the right organizations, ask your friends. Go on the Internet. Look for organizations that cater to your ideal targets. Find out if they provide comfortable opportunities for meeting and interacting with members. Look for opportunities such as committees you can join, publications you can write for, and events where you can speak and network.

Tip 8: Write an Article

If you plan to write an article, identify some topics and some potential publications. Set some time aside to get started. You don't have to write the whole article at once. Work in short time increments. Write down some thoughts. Do some research. Create an outline. But get started. Once you get started, it will become easier to maintain the momentum.

Tip 9: Do Public Speaking

Speaking is one of the most effective techniques for meeting new people and communicating value. If you would like to speak, think of some topics and some potential groups to speak in front of. Call those organizations and pitch your speech.

If you are reluctant to speak because of the fear of embarrassment but still want to pursue it, take steps to overcome your fear. Take classes. Join Toastmasters. Practice in front of audiences that are not threatening. Write a speech that gives great value to your audience. The more confident you are that your speech will be perceived as valuable; the more comfortable you will feel in delivering your speech.

Tip 10: Purchase Contact Management Software

Once you meet qualified targets, don't let them slip away. Maintain a consistent and positive presence in their lives so that when the timing is right, they will be thinking of you.

Research software for contact mailing lists and contact management. Install it, learn how to use it, and keep it updated.

Tip 11: Create Realistic Standards for Measuring Success

Selling is often a long-term process. It takes time to meet the right people and build relationships. And, there is an element of luck. The timing has to be right. So, while your ultimate goal is to bring business in the door, if this is your only measurement of success, you are going to get frustrated. You need to give yourself credit for achieving intermediary successes. For example, if you are trying to do public speaking, this takes several steps. You have to identify places to speak. You have to pick a topic. You have to get approved. You have to write the speech. Each accomplishment brings you closer to your ultimate objective.

We recommend measuring results based upon the following:

Number of tasks completed

If you are completing tasks and doing more than were previously that is a sign of success.

Size of contact data base

If your database is expanding with qualified targets, then this is another milestone that will inevitably lead to more business.

Attitudes about selling

If you are feeling more comfortable with selling, then this too is a way of measuring success. The more comfortable you feel, the more likely you are to feel motivated to do more.

Tip 12: Create a Selling File

Your strategic plan may begin as a simple one-sheet page that outlines your plans. But, over time, as you grow in your awareness and comfort, you will come up with new ideas and tasks. We recommend that as you think of ideas, that you write them down and keep them in a selling project file. Having a file with all of your thoughts and tasks will keep you organized.

Check off when you have completed tasks. If you are working on long-term projects, keep track of the intermediate steps and check them off as accomplished. Each project should have its own sheet of paper so that it is easy to track what needs to be done.

Tip 13: Do a Daily Review

As we mentioned in Chapter 1, the more consistent, constructive attention you give to your selling effort, the more likely you are to succeed. Remember the formula for success: AAMAS.

Attention → Awareness → Motivation → Action → Success

The formula begins with your attention. The more attention, the more awareness of ideas you develop. Awareness of ideas leads to motivation to take action. And, action leads to success.

As part of your strategic plan, we recommend that you commit a minimum of five minutes each day, preferably first thing in the morning when you have more energy, to review your marketing tasks.

Five minutes may not seem like a lot, but it will make a huge difference. These five minutes of review will help you stay focused on selling. It will remind you of tasks that need to be completed. Instead of taking five minutes to walk to the end of the hall to get a cup of coffee, you may elect to use those five minutes to make a phone call to some promising target.

These five minutes also help you to be more alert to selling opportunities throughout the day. In Chapter 1, we pointed out that selling opportunities are often all around you. You may talk with people during the day that could provide entrée to new opportunities. You may read journals that provide ideas for articles or speeches. The more your mind develops the habit of thinking about selling, the more likely you are to notice opportunities if and when they present themselves.

A five-minute review is wonderful habit. But, until the habit is formed, you will need to remind yourself to do it. Put it in your calendar for every day over the course of a month. Right now, you are in the habit of not thinking about selling so unless it is written in your calendar you won't remember it.

Tip 14: Create Accountability

To stay motivated, we recommend that you incorporate accountability into your strategic plan. Select someone you trust who you will report to. These reporting sessions should be done at least monthly. The more frequently you report, the more attention you will give to selling.

No matter how enthusiastic you may be about a particular selling strategy, the fact is that you get busy and may forget about it. Or, your old anti-selling sentiments resurface and cause you to lose interest. Being accountable to someone helps you stay focused and remember your reasons for taking action.

Conclusion

It is helpful to have a strategic plan. But, remember that planning without action has little value. It is easy to write down a bunch of selling strategies. What is more difficult is to develop the willingness to implement selling activities, and to give selling your consistent, constructive attention. To develop this willingness, it is imperative that you identify tasks that keep you in your comfort zone.

A Closing Thought

WE HOPE THAT YOU HAVE FOUND this book useful and interesting.

Selling is important. It can bring you many benefits: more money, power, prestige, better clientele, more friends, enhanced self-esteem, intellectual stimulation, emotional fulfillment, and fun. But, if you are uncomfortable with selling, you may be skeptical about your ability to enjoy these benefits.

In this book, we have strived to help you overcome your discomfort. We have given you strategies for selling in your comfort zone:

- Develop confidence in your ability to offer value
- Identify targets in your comfort zone
- Communicate value to your targets
- Reveal your interest in doing business
- Find comfortable techniques for meeting new people
- Develop comfortable systems to stay in touch

We have given you 106 tips for making the following skills more safe and effective:

- Public speaking
- Seminars
- Public relations
- Documenting the value that you offer
- Satisfaction surveys
- Working a room
- Time management
- Strategic planning

Don't let your discomfort be a barrier any longer. Don't allow your fears and past experiences stop you from identifying the activities within your comfort zone. It is not your lack the capability, but rather your discomfort that stops you. If you are smart, persistent, and have the proper guidance, you can overcome the obstacles and learn how to sell.

Table of Exhibits

Index

0

Selected Books from . . .
THE ABA LAW PRACTICE MANAGEMENT SECTION

The Legal Career Guide:
From Law Student to Lawyer,
Fifth Edition
By Gary A. Munneke and Ellen Wayne

This is a step-by-step guide for planning a law career, preparing and executing a job search, and moving into the market. Whether you're considering a solo career, examining government or corporate work, joining a medium or large firm, or focusing on an academic career, this book is filled with practical advice that will help you find your personal niche in the legal profession. This book will also help you make the right choices in building resumes, making informed career decisions, and taking the first step toward career success.

Women-at-Law: Lessons Learned Along the Pathways to Success
By Phyllis Horn Epstein

Discover how women lawyers in a wide variety of practice settings are meeting the challenges of competing in an often all-consuming profession without sacrificing their desire for a multidimensional life. Women-at-Law provides a wealth of practical guidance and direction from experienced women lawyers who share their life stories and advice to inspire and encourage others by offering solutions to the challenges—personal and professional. You'll learn that, with some effort, a motivated woman can redirect her career, her home life, and her interests, in the long journey that is a successful life. If you are a law student, a practicing lawyer, or simply a woman considering a career

The Lawyer's Guide to Balancing Life and Work, Second Edition
By George W. Kaufman

This newly updated and revised Second Edition is written specifically to help lawyers achieve professional and personal satisfaction in their career. Writing with warmth and seasoned wisdom, George Kaufman examines how the profession has changed over the last five year, then offers philosophical approaches, practical examples, and valuable exercises to help lawyers reconcile their goals and expectations with the realities and demands of the legal profession. Interactive exercises are provided throughout the text and on the accompanying CD, to help you discover how to reclaim your life. New lawyers, seasoned veterans, and those who have personal relationships to lawyers will all benefit from this insightful book.

How to Build and Manage a
Personal Injury Practice, Second Edition
By K. William Gibson

Written exclusively for personal injury practitioners, this indispensable resource explores everything from choosing the right office space to measuring results of your marketing campaign. Author Bill Gibson has carefully constructed this "how-to" manual—highlighting all the tactics, technology, and practical tools necessary for a profitable practice, including how to write a sound business plan, develop an accurate financial forecast, maximize your staff while minimizing costs, and more.

How to Build and Manage an
Entertainment Law Practice
By Gary Greenberg

This book addresses a variety of issues critical to establishing a successful entertainment law practice including getting started, preparing a business plan, getting your foot in the door, creating the right image, and marketing your entertainment law practice. The book discusses the basic differences between entertainment law and other types of law practice and provides guidance for avoiding common pitfalls. In addition, an extensive appendix contains sample agreements, forms, letters, and checklists common to entertainment law practitioners. Includes a diskette containing the essential appendix templates, forms and checklists for easy implementation!

How to Build and Manage an Estates Practice,
Second Edition
By Daniel B. Evans

Whether you aim to define your "niche" in estates law, or market your estates practice on the Internet, this valuable guide can help you make a practice a success. Chapters are logically organized to lead you through the essential stages of developing your specialty practice and include practical, proven advice for everything from organizing estate planning and trust administration files . . . to conducting estate planning interviews . . . to implementing alternative billing strategies . . . to managing your workload (and staff!). Appendices include such sample documents as: an estate planning fee agreement, an estate administration fee agreement, an estate administration schedule, will execution instructions, and more.

ABA LawPracticeManagementSection
MARKETING • MANAGEMENT • TECHNOLOGY • FINANCE

The Successful Lawyer: Powerful Strategies for Transforming Your Practice
By Gerald A. Riskin
Available as a Book, Audio-CD Set, or Combination Package!
Global management consultant and trusted advisor to many of the world's largest law firms, Gerry Riskin goes beyond simple concept or theory and delivers a book packed with practical advice that you can implement right away. By using the principles found in this book, you can live out your dreams, embrace success, and awaken your firm to its full potential. Large law firm or small, managing partners and associates in every area of practice—all can benefit from the information contained in this book. With this book, you can attract what you need and desire into your life, get more satisfaction from your practice and your clients, and do so in a systematic, achievable way.

How to Start and Build a Law Practice, Platinum Fifth Edition
By Jay G Foonberg
This classic ABA bestseller has been used by tens of thousands of lawyers as the comprehensive guide to planning, launching, and growing a successful practice. It's packed with over 600 pages of guidance on identifying the right location, finding clients, setting fees, managing your office, maintaining an ethical and responsible practice, maximizing available resources, upholding your standards, and much more. You'll find the information you need to successfully launch your practice, run it at maximum efficiency, and avoid potential pitfalls along the way. If you're committed to starting—and growing—your own practice, this one book will give you the expert advice you need to make it succeed for years to come.

The Lawyer's Field Guide to Effective Business Development
By William J. Flannery, Jr.
This book is much more than a "survival guide"— it is a "success guide." Having trained more than 10,000 lawyers from around the world in client relationship management, business development and effective communication skills, William J. Flannery, an ex-IBM executive and J.D., focuses on practical ideas and approaches for business growth and relationship improvement. Flannery's approach to winning and retaining long-term, attractive clients is detailed and sensible. He proves that with the right approaches, the appropriate homework and diligence, and a little bit of courage, any lawyer can not only be smart, but effective as a client relationship manager and advocate.

The Law Firm Associate's Guide to Personal Marketing and Selling Skills
By Catherine Alman MacDonagh and Beth Marie Cuzzone
This is the first volume in ABA's new groundbreaking Law Firm Associates Development Series, created to teach important skills that associates and other lawyers need to succeed at their firms, but that they may have not learned in law school. This volume focuses on personal marketing and sales skills. It covers creating a personal marketing plan, finding people within your target market, preparing for client meetings, "asking" for business, realizing marketing opportunities, keeping your clients, staying in touch with your network inside and outside the firm, and more. An accompanying trainer's manual illustrating how to best structure the sessions and use the book is available to firms to facilitate group training sessions.

Many law firms expect their new associates to hit the ground running when they are hired on. Although firms often take the time to bring these associates up to speed on client matters, they can be reluctant to invest the time needed to train them how to improve personal skills such as marketing. This book will serve as a brief, easy-to-digest primer for associates on how to develop and use marketing and selling techniques.

The Lawyer's Guide to Marketing Your Practice, Second Edition
Edited by James A. Durham and Deborah McMurray
This book is packed with practical ideas, innovative strategies, useful checklists, and sample marketing and action plans to help you implement a successful, multi-faceted, and profit-enhancing marketing plan for your firm. Organized into four sections, this illuminating resource covers: Developing Your Approach; Enhancing Your Image; Implementing Marketing Strategies and Maintaining Your Program. Appendix materials include an instructive primer on market research to inform you on research methodologies that support the marketing of legal services. The accompanying CD-ROM contains a wealth of checklists, plans, and other sample reports, questionnaires, and templates—all designed to make implementing your marketing strategy as easy as possible!

The Busy Lawyer's Guide to Success: Essential Tips to Power Your Practice
By Reid F. Trautz and Dan Pinnington
Busy lawyers do not have dozens of extra hours to conduct research looking for new tips and ideas to streamline and enhance their practice of law. They need "just-in-time" learning to acquire the knowledge necessary to build their practices. This convenient pocket guide is the "best ever" collection of practical tips, ideas, and techniques to help you survive, thrive, and find success in the practice of law.

30-Day Risk-Free Order Form
Call Today! 1-800-285-2221
Monday–Friday, 7:30 AM – 5:30 PM, Central Time

Qty	Title	LPM Price	Regular Price	Total
_____	The Legal Career Guide: From Law Student to Lawyer, Fifth Edition (5110479)	$ 29.95	$ 34.95	$_____
_____	Women-at-Law: Lessons Learned Along the Pathways to Success (5110509)	39.95	49.95	$_____
_____	The Lawyer's Guide to Balancing Life and Work, Second Edition (5110566)	29.95	39.95	$_____
_____	How to Build and Manage a Personal Injury Practice, Second Edition (5110575)	54.95	64.95	$_____
_____	How to Build and Manage an Entertainment Law Practice (5110453)	54.95	64.95	$_____
_____	How to Build and Manage an Estates Practice, Second Edition (5110421)	44.95	54.95	$_____
_____	The Successful Lawyer—Book Only (5110531)	64.95	84.95	$_____
_____	The Successful Lawyer—Audio CDs Only (5110532)	129.95	149.95	$_____
_____	The Successful Lawyer—Audio CDs/Book Combination (5110533)	174.95	209.95	$_____
_____	How to Start and Build a Law Practice, Platinum Fifth Edition (5110508)	57.95	69.95	$_____
_____	The Lawyer's Field Guide to Effective Business Development (5110578)	49.95	59.95	$_____
_____	The Law Firm Associate's Guide to Personal Marketing and Selling Skills (5110582)	39.95	49.95	$_____
_____	The Lawyer's Guide to Marketing Your Practice, Second Edition (5110500)	79.95	89.95	$_____
_____	The Busy Lawyer's Guide to Success: Essential Tips to Power Your Practice (5110687)	44.95	69.95	$_____

*Postage and Handling	
$10.00 to $24.99	$5.95
$25.00 to $49.99	$9.95
$50.00 to $99.99	$12.95
$100.00 to $349.99	$17.95
$350 to $499.99	$24.95

**Tax
DC residents add 5.75%
IL residents add 10.25%

*Postage and Handling $_____
**Tax $_____
TOTAL $_____

PAYMENT

❑ Check enclosed (to the ABA)

❑ Visa   ❑ MasterCard   ❑ American Express

Account Number   Exp. Date   Signature

Name _____ Firm _____
Address _____
City _____ State _____ Zip _____
Phone Number _____ E-Mail Address _____

Note: E-Mail address is required if ordering the
The Lawyer's Guide to Fact Finding on the Internet
E-mail Newsletter (5110498)

Guarantee
If—for any reason—you are not satisfied with your purchase, you may
return it within 30 days of receipt for a complete refund of the price of the
book(s). No questions asked!

Mail: ABA Publication Orders, P.O. Box 10892, Chicago, Illinois 60610-0892
♦ Phone: 1-800-285-2221 ♦ FAX: 312-988-5568

E-Mail: abasvcctr@abanet.org ♦ Internet: http://www.lawpractice.org/catalog

About the CD

The accompanying CD contains valuable forms, worksheets, and checklists from *Selling in Your Comfort Zone: Safe and Effective Strategies for Developing New Business.* The files are in Microsoft Word® format.

For additional information about the files on the CD, please open and read the "**readme.doc**" file on the CD.

NOTE: The set of files on the CD may only be used on a single computer or moved to and used on another computer. Under no circumstances may the set of files be used on more than one computer at one time. If you are interested in obtaining a license to use the set of files on a local network, please contact: Director, Copyrights and Contracts, American Bar Association, 321 N. Clark Street, Chicago, IL 60654, (312) 988-6101. **Please read the license and warranty statements on the following page before using this CD.**

CD-ROM to accompany
Selling in Your Comfort Zone: Safe and Effective Strategies for Developing New Business